T0303136

Travels with My Father

Travels with My Father

Life, Death, and
a Psychic Detective

Nancy Myer

GoodKnight Books
Pittsburgh, Pennsylvania

GoodKnight Books

© 2013 by Nancy E. Myer

Published by GoodKnight Books, an imprint of Paladin Communications, Pittsburgh, Pennsylvania

Printed in the United States of America

First Edition

Library of Congress Control Number: 2013945746

ISBN 978-0-9885025-0-5

The names of some people and locations in this book have been fictionalized to protect privacy.

This book is dedicated to Harriet and Fredric Myer, who taught me that love is a vital ingredient to our survival.

The winter of our loved ones' lives
Comes long before we are ready.
Busy with the day to day of life,
We fail to see the frost when first it shows.
As the snows come and the grip is harder,
We are forced to notice its advance.
But oh, the final vicious blizzard
That takes our special loved one . . .
We are so unprepared for.

—Nancy Myer

Contents

Travels with My Father

Prologue

One thing I'm sure of is that I see life differently than others do. I'm used to it by now, but most people don't easily understand the differences and how those differences affect me and those around me.

As far back as I can remember, I knew things I had no logical reason to know. I traveled all over the world as I was growing up because my dad was in the U.S. Foreign Service, and people assumed that my life experiences explained the extra knowledge. I knew that wasn't it. Things have always popped into my head—information that turned out to be right—but I never had a logical explanation for why I knew it.

When my family was living in Chile and I was about eight, I asked my father why I could do this and no one else could. "What's wrong with me, Daddy?" I asked.

"Nothing at all, Nance," he said. "God just gave you extra gifts. I know there are other people like you. It doesn't happen very often, but it does happen. I have a little bit of it too, but nothing like what you have. Don't be afraid of your gift—use it to help people. When you're not sure about it and wonder if you're okay, just remember that God made you this way so He must need you for something important."

I remember we sat quietly at the side of a field and looked at the view. I wasn't exactly sure what he meant because I was too young to understand. But if he said it was okay, then I wasn't going to worry about it.

Life is full of wonderful mysteries that no one understands, one in particular being what happens after death. People who have died often reveal to me information about unresolved issues that I can pass on to their families. I help to locate missing wills—and missing people's bodies. Sometimes, this incredible help from the other side of death reveals murderers to me. This is how life unfolds for me. Through my job, my experiences, and the many accounts I've heard from others of loved ones reaching back across the divide, I have become certain that love survives death.

With the experiences I have had, I shouldn't have been surprised when my father showed up in my living room chair one day. It was after his funeral, and he acted as if it were the most normal thing in the world to have a chat with me at my house. I was just as surprised as anyone might be who experiences this kind of communication. I was also full of questions, and Dad was my companion on a journey to find the answers.

This book is about a psychic woman's struggle to survive grief, deal with a rapidly expanding gift, and comprehend some incredible events. It's also the story of my father's extraordinary love for his family.

I want to share what I have learned on my travels with my father to help others answer their own questions. The perspective of someone like me, who is well known for being down to earth and direct, might make it easier for people—for you, perhaps—to accept communications from loved ones who have passed on.

If you have experienced incredible visits from the other side, you are not alone. You and I and many others can celebrate this part of life with the joyful awareness that death does not stop love.

Chapter 1

A Surprise Visit

I sat at the dining room table just after breakfast with a lap full of squirming Blake as I tried to put shoes on his feet. My son's baby shoes were critical because I kept track of what he was up to through the jingle of the bells on his shoelace covers. This kept his mayhem to a minimum. Blake couldn't be bothered with this ritual and tried to undo the laces as quickly as I tied them, but their double knots defeated him. I deftly slid the covers over the laces, and he giggled at the musical sound his feet now made.

"Down now, Ma!" he dictated.

His feet churned madly in the air as I lifted him to the floor, and then he took off in his toddler run. Jingle, jingle, jingle. The inevitable tumble followed, as his balance could not keep up with his attempts for speed.

"Uh-oh," he chortled as he brushed his hands off. Jingle, jingle, jingle straight for the powder room door. "No, no, no," he said seriously. "Bad boy, Bake." Shaking his head side to side and repeating his self-admonishment, he struggled with the childproof doorknob cover in an attempt to gain entry to the powder room. "Ma, hep," he called to me. "I need fishin'."

"Oh no, you don't," I said. "You know you're not allowed to go fishing in the toilet." I pretended to read the morning newspaper while I watched his antics. After the physical and emotional stress I had endured with six miscarriages, I was now immersed in being the mother of this delightful urchin that my husband and I had adopted, and I was enjoying every bit of it.

"But, Ma, I need dis," he said, running to me as fast as his stubby legs would carry him and hugging my leg as hard as he could. "I need dis!"

"Mommy said no. Mommy does not want you to get in trouble again."

He folded his little arms across his chest and gave me his best 17-month-old glare. I struggled not to laugh, knowing that would make things worse. "Mommy said no, Blake, and you know I won't change my mind. Now go play with your toys." One more stubborn glare accompanied a jingling stamp of his little foot. He looked down and then peered up under his lashes with his best smile. When that didn't work either, he went over to his toy box and pulled out every toy. Baby's revenge.

I went back to reading a newspaper article about the Apollo 14 astronauts, who recently had landed on the moon. It was about a ceremony for them. I still couldn't believe that men actually had walked on the moon. Suddenly, I realized the room was silent. No jingles. Then I heard Blake muttering to himself, "No, no, no. Bad boy, Bake."

I had been so engrossed in the news story that I didn't hear him walk right by me headed for the doorway to the kitchen. He was peering over the bookcase that blocked that door and trying to rock it back and forth to move it, all the while telling himself, "No, no, no. Bad boy, Bake."

"Blake, leave that alone," I said as I hurried up to retrieve him. He was getting strong enough to wiggle the bookcase, and I didn't want him to realize that he could manage that. My mind flashed back to the time when I turned my back for a moment and nine-month-old Blake had suddenly vanished. The scare he put me through! I remembered my frantic search all over the first floor of the house. My beagle George started hunting for him too and went directly into the kitchen, where the dog started throwing himself against the oven door and howling at the top of his lungs. I rushed into the kitchen to find Blake inside the oven and waving through the window in the oven door. He had turned the oven dial and his bare toe was a millimeter from the red-hot element. I snatched him out of the oven, and not thinking that he couldn't talk, I yelled, "What on earth were you doing?"

I was stunned when he answered, "I cookin'!" He was too smart for his own good and quick as lightning, even though he couldn't yet walk. I never found out how he got into that oven, but his father and I made sure it never happened again. We blocked the kitchen entry with a small bookcase, heavy with cookbooks, and shut the louvered doors on the other entrance, securing them with child-proof locks on the handles. After that incident he was never again allowed in the kitchen unsupervised. We wondered who the idiot was who invented a stove with the controls on the front in easy reach of any curious toddler. Until Blake did that, we never realized how dangerous those burner controls were. Of course, I could probably pack the kitchen with kids, and only Blake would bother the stove controls.

I was glad that I wasn't trying to work while raising my son; I was lucky enough to have the time to enjoy him and to make sure he survived his early childhood. Blake was always getting into scrapes, and my husband and I joked that if he made it to five alive, we would have a huge party. I nicknamed him Mr. Mischief and a lot of my neighbors called him that too as they saw me running after him. His escapades provided great entertainment for everyone.

Halloween was about to arrive, and I had decided to make his costume from scratch. I had started sewing recently and was really enjoying it. I couldn't find a pattern I liked so, using his overalls for size, I created a little camel-colored, one-piece corduroy outfit with big leather buttons taken from an old overcoat. With orange and yellow rickrack on the cuffs of the sleeves and pants, he looked like an adorable little gingerbread boy with big brown eyes and curly black hair. Blake especially loved the pockets. Whenever he tried it on, he would spend a long time sticking his hands in them, which would keep him busy for a while.

I heard my dad's familiar whistle outside my front door. Five clear notes: Zip-a-dee-doo-dah. Blake heard the whistling too and ran as fast as he could to peer through the mail slot. I heard Dad's chuckle as Blake stuck his little fingers through the slot. "Hi, Dampa. You comin' here?"

"I certainly am," said my father. "Go get Mommy to open the door."

I swung open the heavy door to receive a bear hug from my dad. "I was supposed to go to a luncheon," he said, "but it was canceled, so I figured I'd come over here and have some fun with you guys." My parents lived in Dover, about 50 miles away from my home in Newark, Delaware. As Blake stood next to my father, he held his arms up and opened and shut his hands to let Dad know he was ready to be picked up. Dad slyly handed me a Blake-sized red wheelbarrow over my son's head. I took the toy and shoved it out of sight around the corner. Dad scooped up Blake and held him high, flying him around the room like an airplane as they both giggled away. Dad placed Blake carefully on his feet, making sure he had his balance before letting go, and then plopped down in his favorite chair in the living room.

Blake tore through his toys, looking for just the right thing to share with Dampa, while Dad motioned me to hand back the toy wheelbarrow, which he then set on the floor. Blake had a block in each hand when he turned to Dampa. He spied the wheelbarrow and stopped short, prowled over, and circled it suspiciously. "Dampa, dat for me?"

Dad said, "Well, that depends. We have to see if it's the right size."

"How we do dat?" Blake was now dancing with excitement.

Dad positioned Blake between the handles and carefully showed him how to hold and push the wheelbarrow. Off Blake went as if he had known how to use it all along. He stopped to pick up toys and delighted at the clang his blocks made when he tossed them in the wheelbarrow. He pushed it around for a while, then suddenly ran to Dampa and climbed into his lap, taking Dad's face in his hands and staring into his eyes as he said quite seriously, "I wuv you, Dampa, and I thankin' you for dat bawwo." He slithered off Dad's lap and ran back to the wheelbarrow.

"Well," said Dad, "if you're going to have a rascal, you might as well have a charming one." We laughed as we watched Blake tooling around the living room with his toys in the wheelbarrow. He quickly learned to balance it so the toys didn't fall out. As he bent to pick up his favorite book, he looked over at Dad with a mischievous grin.

Blake plopped the book in my father's lap and pointed to the turtle on the cover. "Dampa, dis a duck," he said. Dad settled Blake in his lap, and they played their favorite game.

As happy as I was with my child, Mother and Dad were even happier. As the head of vocational agriculture for the State of Delaware, my father had frequent meetings in Newark at the university, and Mother usually came with him. Sometimes he dropped her off at my house, and sometimes she waited around and they would meet for lunch or visit friends. They always enjoyed being together. They were doting grandparents and often dropped in to play with their mischievous grandson. Mother had a meeting today, so it was just Dad who stopped by. Blake and Dad sat together in the big armchair and chattered away. Dad was teaching Blake the names of animals, but it wasn't going well because Blake decided that every animal was a duck. With the book open in his lap, Dad turned the pages saying, "Cow . . . horse . . .," and right behind the correct word for the animal, Blake affirmed, "Duck!" while pointing at each picture.

As usual, Blake quickly tired of sitting still, slid to the floor, and ran to pick up his rubber ducky. "See, Dampa, dis my duck."

"Right you are," Dad said, laughing. "That certainly is a duck."

"Wubba ducky, he da one," Blake proudly sang. "Ma moosic pease." My father groaned as I pulled the rubber ducky record, a well-worn 45, out of its sleeve and placed it on the turntable. Leaving my dad to sing the rubber ducky song with Blake, I went into the kitchen to make sandwiches. I enjoyed listening to their happy chatter as they finally settled on turtle-duck, cow-duck and so on.

Dad airplaned Blake to his highchair and strapped him in. I affixed a large bib because Blake was a messy eater. George the beagle, a veteran of Blake's meals in that highchair, took up his post below the chair to clean up whatever might fall. Blake chattered on as Dad and I visited. Dad pulled a small gift box out of his pocket to show me what he'd gotten Mother. It was a silver University of Delaware key.

"She'll love that, Dad," I said with admiration.

"I ordered it before graduation," he said, "but it took a while to get here. I picked it up today after the meeting. I am so proud of your mother for completing her Masters, and I want to thank you for helping me talk her into it. She's so talented, and I think she's beginning to realize how good she is."

Some of the paintings that Mom had done for her thesis were put on display at the art department of the university, and this had helped to supply her with some needed self-confidence.

He thought a moment. "She's painting more and she's getting better and better. She's made a lot of new friends who are artists too. I love seeing her enjoying herself."

Dad thought some more, his look far off. "I think I made the right decision leaving the Foreign Service when I did. I had this horrible feeling I wouldn't survive another tour of duty. I couldn't stand the idea of her being alone at a time like that. At least back here if something happens, you can get to her quickly." Then he mentioned that he and Mom were driving to Newport News over the upcoming weekend to see his father—my grandfather—and Aunt Alice and Uncle Johnny, Dad's sister and brother-in-law.

"Grandpa Elsie's not doing well," Dad continued, still with that distant gaze in his eyes. "I think I need to see him. We'll be back on Monday."

A chill went through me when he talked about coming back Monday. Somewhere inside me I knew that was not going to happen. I shifted my eyes from his so he wouldn't see the pain this thought produced.

I could tell he knew something was wrong, but he didn't pursue it and I didn't volunteer anything. I was not at all ready to face the thought of losing my father. I shook the feeling off and busied myself clearing the dishes. Once in a while I would get feelings like this, that something was going to happen, but they weren't detailed in any way, so I would never quite be sure about what was coming. I tried to reassure myself that I was misinterpreting this sudden impression, and that the insistent feeling that he would not be back on Monday was nothing more than needless worry.

Through the haze of my thoughts, I heard him say, "I'd better get going. Your mother and I have to pack for the trip and I want to give her my present." He grabbed me in another big hug, then he looked me square in the eye. "Take good care of her for me." He looked at me silently for a moment, a look full of love. Then he added, "I'm very proud of you."

Before I could comprehend and react, he was gone. I stood at the door with Blake in my arms and waved goodbye. Tears welled as the reality hit me that Dad was getting the same information I was. My father was going to die, and soon, and we both knew it. Over the years I've found it an agonizing part of having the abilities that I do: knowing when someone I love is going to die. Yet, I'd rather know in advance than get blindsided by it, and now as Dad walked away, I felt a big hole growing inside me.

Tears streamed down my face. I closed the door, placed Blake on the floor, and fell into the big armchair, still warm from his presence. Nausea overwhelmed me, and I sobbed uncontrollably. My dad was going to die.

Disturbed by my crying, Blake patted my face, and then he grabbed a little fistful of tissues and tried to wipe away my tears. His frightened, pinched expression forced me to get control of my thoughts and take him in my arms. We rocked together for a bit until I could stop crying. Blake slid down and went to work with his "bawwo" again, and I tried to convince myself that what I knew to be true could not be so. After all, Dad was only 54 and in good health. He'd just had a physical, and told me that the doctor had pronounced him fit. I sensed he wasn't, but I had to stay calm so my crying wouldn't frighten my baby.

A little while later, I put Blake down for a nap, and then still in shock sat absently sewing the last of the rickrack on Blake's Halloween costume. I began to prepare myself for a world without Dad. I felt the inevitability of it along with my own lack of power to prevent it, and I wondered if I would ever get used to this intuition.

Chapter 2

Death Steals into My Life

I was asleep beside my husband at 2:30 on a Saturday morning when the phone rang. I grabbed it knowing something was wrong. It was Mother.

"Your dad's had a heart attack," she told me. "Uncle Johnny drove like a madman to get us to this hospital in Richmond because he says it's the best. Dad's alive but Johnny says there's a lot of damage. They have him stabilized and hooked up to all kinds of machines. Your uncle and I are going back to Newport News to get some sleep, but I wanted you to know. Can you call Susan for me, please?"

I was numb. I was glad they had been with Uncle Johnny. Dad's brother-in-law was a cardiologist and if anyone could save his life, it would be my uncle.

I heard myself say, "I'll call Susan, but what can I do for you? I am so sorry, Mother."

"It was really bad," she said through tears, "and I didn't think he was going to make it." She paused. "There's so much damage. Johnny thinks he won't be able to walk for some time, so I'm going to need your help when we get home."

"Of course," I told her. "I'll help you in any way I can. You know that." I supported her line of reasoning while on the inside feeling as if it had been written in stone that he wasn't going to survive. I wanted to drive down and see him but I had never driven that far by myself, and I had the baby to take care of. I hung up the phone and went downstairs quietly so my husband could go back to sleep.

I called my sister, Susan. I could barely think what to say to her. Part of me clung to hope that the worst was over and that Dad would beat the odds. The intuitive part of me knew the awful truth, and that I kept to myself.

Five or six hours later Mother called again. My husband was at work, and Blake was taking a nap. Mother was crying so hard she could hardly get the words out.

"Nance, he didn't make it. He died so peacefully, he didn't even set off the alarms on the monitors." Miles apart, we cried together that the most wonderful, loving man in our lives was gone.

My mind went to practical things, like what would she do next. "Are you going to stay with Aunt Alice for a while?" I asked.

"No," said Mother. "Alice is driving up to Dover with me tonight. She's going to help me with the funeral arrangements. You have to re-member, this is her only brother who just died, and eight months ago she lost her mother. She's having a hard time too."

I asked what I could do to help.

She paused. "Can you come down to Dover to help me plan the fu-neral?"

"I'll be there for you," I said at once. "But I'll have to bring Blake with me, and you know how full of mischief he is."

I could hear a tired smile in her voice. "That's okay. He'll remind us that we have to go on."

I got off the phone and realized that I would have to get to Dover be-fore she did. She would be arriving at the house after dark, and there wouldn't be a light on in the place. I couldn't let that happen. I quickly washed a load of clothes for Blake and me. I'd need something dressy to wear to the viewings and to the funeral.

The only other family funeral I had been to was Dad's mother's fu-neral the previous March. All the other family deaths occurred when we were overseas, which had made it a little unreal to me, and as a kid, I was not as aware as I was now of the pain and suffering involved. This was going to be horrible.

When my husband got back from teaching, he took the car to fill it with gas. He also helped me load the playpen, port-a-crib, and all the other stuff I would need for Blake. Of all the days for Dad to die, Halloween was not a good pick. I had never liked the holiday because I was afraid of ghosts.

I had dressed Blake in his costume, and he looked adorable. He was carrying a little plastic pumpkin, and my neighbors came over to give him some candy and to try to help me where they could. I walked Blake around our street so he could enjoy a little trick-or-treating, and then I put him in his car seat and off we went. He chattered happily until the motion of the car put him to sleep.

I did indeed beat Mom home. I grabbed Blake, rushed inside, and dashed through the big Victorian, turning lights on in every room. I was breathless from completing my task when I heard car doors. I walked out the back door with Blake still in my arms to greet Mother and Aunt Alice.

When Mother saw me, she said, "How on earth did you know?"

"How did I know what?" I asked.

Aunt Alice said, "All the way up your mother talked about being worried to see the house all dark, yet when we pulled in, you had the house ablaze with light!"

Mother looked up at the lighted windows. "I knew it had to be you. Thank you." She hugged Blake and me together, and Blake wrapped his little arms around her neck and would not let go.

"Yook, Danma, I gots Haddoween!" Blake said. He scrambled down to the ground so that he could dance around and show her his gingerbread boy costume. For a moment we could laugh at his antics, but sadness returned as we helped each other unpack the cars.

As soon as Dad's obituary hit the papers, phone calls and visits began, and the mailman brought armloads of cards. Mother did her best to speak with everyone and visit with the people who came to the door. She understood better than I how well known and loved Dad was. Visitor after visitor shared stories of wonderful things Dad had done for them. Everyone was devastated because he was so young and it had happened so suddenly.

Susan and her family had arrived by now. Mother was running on adrenaline, and Susan and I forced her to lie down every now and then. My sister and I took over greeting visitors, but Mother couldn't rest for long, and she would come back to the Victorian front parlor to greet friends and strangers who came to pay their respects. I realized that on some level this helped her to hold onto Dad for a little longer.

For me it was an exhausting haze of faces, as I struggled to take care of Blake. Susan's daughter, Tracy, was a month older than Blake and a handful as well. The day-to-day care of our children helped Susan and me get through the procession of mourners and the funeral plans. Blake's enthusiasm for his cousin, who was as tiny as he was big, was hardly welcomed by Tracy. At first, every time he came near her she screamed, leaving Blake in tears, but gradually he won her over until they finally began to play together.

The funeral home sat next door to Mother's house, and the director was a family friend. When we opened the door to walk over for the funeral we found that the Future Farmers of America students from all over Delaware had formed an honor guard to guide us from Mother's front door to the entrance of the funeral home. Mother looked at me, smiled, and squared her shoulders as she made her way through the lines of young people. Because of Dad's important role in vocational agriculture the last few years, these young people—many of whom he had helped personally—came to honor his whole life as a teacher in Delaware and in countries all over the world. What a truly wonderful thing to do for our family.

As we got close to the funeral home doors, I heard someone call my name. "Miss Nancy, Miss Nancy, please, Miss Nancy." I looked over the heads of the honor guard to see an old African-American man who was near and dear to me. Charles Smack had come to see Daddy off.

I walked through the file of youngsters to Charles' warm embrace. Tears streamed down his cheeks as he looked heavenward and said, "Lord, ya shoulda took me, not my Freddy. Such a good man." Charles had known Dad forever, and had told me many things about my father as a young man. Charles drew me over to a large group of black people, none of whom I recognized. He alluded to three men and said to me, "These gentlemen wants you to know something about your Daddy." To the men he barked, "Go ahead now, stop that blubbering and tell her."

The men stood together crying. One of them drew himself up and said through his tears, "Miss Nancy, if it weren't for your daddy being so brave, I'd be dead long time ago." The group of people that stood behind this man said, "Amen."

I was stunned. What was he talking about?

Charles picked up the story. "When these men," and he indicated all three, "were younger, they worked with your father in the fields and on the chicken farms. At different times for reasons no one can never understand, they run afoul of the Klan." A group of voices from behind Charles said, "Mm-hmmm."

"Each time when the Klan was fixin' to hang someone," Charles went on, "we'd run get your daddy. He'd come runnin' with his little .22, and he talk those bad men out of killing these fellows." He gestured toward the large group of people. "All of these folks are here today to honor your daddy because he save the lives of these three men. And we all jus' broken up because he dies so young."

Dumbfounded does not begin to describe how I felt. Ever since Dad's death was announced in the papers, we had heard wonderful stories of how he brought food to people who had nothing and how he helped others get jobs. Accounts of his kindness came to us as a gift from so many people as they shared in our grieving. But nothing approaching this story would ever have occurred to me. Dad had never said a word about it.

Charles laughed, "I knew it, he never told nobody because he was afraid of what Emma would do to him if she found out he was opposing the Klan."

I laughed through my tears. "Yes," I said, "my grandmother would surely have pitched a royal fit if she had known." We all laughed at the memory of Dad's cantankerous mother.

Charles introduced me to each of the men Dad saved, and they introduced their wives, children, even some grandchildren.

"Your Daddy made all this possible," Charles said.

It was an eerie feeling, overwhelming really, thinking that many of these lovely adults and children wouldn't be alive if Dad had not been dangerously courageous.

I thanked them all for coming and apologized for having to leave to go inside the funeral home. I said to the group, "You have given me a wonderful gift by showing me what my father did. I've always been proud of him, but never more than I am right now, looking at all of you and knowing he had such a role in your lives."

The mother of one of the men, an elderly, frail woman, pointed at Blake, still in my arms. The woman said to me, "You're like your Daddy. You don't care nothin' about society's barriers."

Blake was smiling and talking to everyone; his lovely brown eyes, coffee-and-milk complexion, and soft curls announced his mixed heritage. He had just learned to clap and happily took the moment to show everyone. They clapped back to him and all smiled through their tears to see this happy grandchild of the man they loved. I knew that they had traveled a long way to pay their respects to my father.

"Yo' daddy mus' be proud of you too," the elderly woman said to me.

"I hope so," I said.

"We know so," said Charles. "Your daddy was always bragging about you kids. Now you go on in, honey, and help your momma."

"Please come inside and join us," I said as I held Charles' hand.

"All of the folks can't fit in there," he said. "We just be here waiting. We come in and say goodbye after the service."

I went in to Dad's funeral service with a whole new perspective on why he had been so concerned about my safety when I adopted a child of mixed race. I remembered his advice: "Always live in a university town, not in the country. Remember, the Klan is alive and well." I knew about his views on prejudice, so at the time he had said this to me, it made no sense. Now I understood why the idea had frightened him.

At the service, Susan and I sat on either side of Mother. The children were on our laps at Mother's request, and their jabbered communication helped her get through the ceremony. After the funeral Mother slept for several hours for the first time since Dad died. She came back downstairs to find Blake trying to teach Tracy the rubber ducky song. She smiled at their antics, but her eyes were empty. She seemed so lost without her Fred.

Chapter 3

The Cranberry Sweater

I folded each of Blake's diapers and flattened them all with slow, deliberate care. I needed to block out the last three weeks. I was only 26 years old and thought I was grown up, but when Dad died I was bereft. He was my friend, my strength, and a person who, like me, had an ability to sense the future. I sought daily to lock the grief inside myself so that I could help Mother survive, but my inexperience with the grieving process showed. Recognizing how she felt didn't help me know what to do. The awful truth was that all I could do was be there to listen.

I had always known that Mother and Dad were an integral part of each other. They could sense each other's needs without saying a word. It was like their fluid, mirrored movement on the dance floor. Both were miserable any time they were forced by life to be apart from each other. Mother always said she was an incomplete person without him, and he said the same about her. Together they were whole.

Mother seemed to slowly die these last weeks. Her eyes were lifeless. She was going through the motions of a now empty life. She ate, she talked, but her eyes never smiled, even with a lapful of Blake.

As strong as I appeared to be for Mother during the day, alone at night I too felt lost and fragile. Dad and I used to talk about how I could sense what was going to happen—things that turned out to be completely accurate. I had relied on his help to understand this overwhelming ability: I could see the future.

Dad had said, "I can't explain to you why it works, Nance, but I know that it does because I can do it too." He said with wonder in his voice, "I don't get the detail you do, but what comes through turns out to be very real." He shrugged. "Darned if I know how it happens, though."

These unique abilities that we shared formed an extra bond between us. Losing the only person I knew who was like me in this respect heightened the terrible sense of aloneness that had weighed me down through long days.

I thought for the thousandth time: How could Dad be gone? He seemed so healthy and he wasn't at all old. He didn't smoke or drink. His work kept him walking everywhere and climbing all over machinery. Boom, just like that, his heart attacked us all and he was gone.

As I sat there folding diapers, a soft whistle in my father's tones cut through my devastated thoughts. Zip-a-dee-doo-dah. I had heard the notes of my father's whistle thousands of times. As I looked up, I heard him chuckle. He sat in his usual gangly sprawl in the gold armchair across the living room from me. I stopped folding, holding the diaper in midair. He wore a ratty old cranberry sweater, one he loved, with black leather patches on the elbows. Mother always seemed to be repairing the stitches around the elbow patches and had so many times threatened to get rid of "that old thing."

His beautiful smile lit up the room, but his eyes contradicted that smile. "Don't cry, Nance," he said. "I'm fine. It's your mother I'm worried about."

I stared in shock at this physical manifestation of my dead father in my living room. Yet, it seemed so natural for him to be there talking to me, especially about Mother. I realized that I still held the last diaper I had been folding. I was afraid to move an inch for fear he would disappear. The child inside me wanted him to stay.

His words hung in the air. I didn't say hello. I didn't ask how this was possible. I said, "I'm worried about her too. She doesn't want to go on without you." My words didn't break the spell; he didn't disappear. I thought, Am I really holding a conversation with my father's ghost?

Pain swept across his face and he shuddered. "You tell her I was here and that she has to go on. She has to be there for all of you because I can't be. You take good care of her for me, okay?"

"I will," I said. "I promise."

His eyes still bore pain. "I'm so sorry this happened. I love you all." And then he was gone as suddenly as he had appeared.

The room once again fell silent. I felt a vacuum lock into the space around the chair after he had vanished. The feeling of his love remained, but his absence drained me. I sat rigid and hugged the stack of clean diapers to my chest as tears poured down my face. I couldn't move. I was frozen in place gripping those darn diapers.

"Okay, I'm losing it with grief," I said out loud, trying to regain some hold on reality. "I just talked to my father's ghost. He talked to me. Is this real?"

My father's whistle sounded again, softly but clear as a bell, next to my right ear.

I said to the empty air, "Is that your way of telling me I'm not nuts?" A rapping sound on the table behind my head startled me. This was no dream. I wanted to do something. I needed to move, to take some action, any action, to reassure myself that I was okay. But I sat completely still, unable to move and feeling the tears that kept pouring down my nose onto the diapers.

My father's ghost had just dropped in for a visit! No matter how hard I tried, I couldn't move. The same rigidity had struck me once before, in high school when I visited the Garden of Gethsemane during a tour of Jordan. I shook off the emotional memory of that day.

How could I explain my father's ghost in the living room talking to me? It had been a normal, everyday kind of a conversation. Somewhere, my father existed in some form, and he had visited me. I sat there in silence, my mind racing.

The ringing of the telephone jolted me to action. For the first time in minutes—or had it been hours?—I was able to move. I picked up the receiver, leery about who might be on the other end. Cautiously, I whispered, "Hello?"

It was my sister, Susan. "Nancy, are you all right?" she asked. "You sound funny."

I had to laugh. "Funny. You think I sound funny? That's quite an understatement."

Susan said, "What's wrong with you?"

I gathered my thoughts. "Susan, something just happened here. The strangest thing. I don't know if you'll . . ." I took a deep breath, and then told her bluntly, "Dad was here in this room. He sat in the chair across from me and talked to me just like he did when he was alive."

There was silence on the other end of the phone, and I could tell that she must be thinking I was crazy or exhausted or dreaming. Instead, she asked softly, "Nancy, are you sure?"

"Of course, I'm sure!" I said. The conviction in my voice surprised me because I hadn't completely believed it, but now I knew Dad really had visited me.

I told Susan, "He had that ratty old cranberry sweater on. You know, the one I asked Mom to give me as a memento. That sweater's upstairs in mothballs, but he had it on."

Susan and I speculated whether the sweater would actually be in the place I had so recently packed it. We agreed that I should go check and she would call me back in a few minutes.

I slammed down the phone and ran upstairs. I opened the zippered bag I had placed the sweater in. There it was, neatly folded with mothballs all around it.

I raced back downstairs as the phone rang.

"It's there," I said breathlessly. "It's right where I put it."

Susan said, "How can he do that?"

"I have no idea," I said.

"You said he talked to you. What did he say?"

I repeated Dad's message about our mother, trying to describe to Susan his sadness and obvious pain at leaving all of us.

"You have to call Mother and tell her," said Susan.

I hesitated. "How can I do that? I don't even know if she would believe me. And if she does, is it going to make her even sadder? She's already so depressed."

"You have to tell her," Susan asserted. "He's come back because he loves her. She has to know." She brought the conversation to a close so I could call Mother.

The phone stared at me from the table, but I had to think this through. What to tell her, how to tell her. What to do if she didn't believe me, or worse, if she had some kind of breakdown on the telephone at the stress of such an announcement.

As I tried to scrape together my nerve, I heard Dad's whistle breaking the silence again. The quick, clear tones of those five notes renewed my tears. I loved the way he whistled, and when I was a little girl, I tried to practice so that someday I could whistle that well too. He could make his whistle warble, shoot high up on the scale, or go low. All I could do was a plain note, but it was clear and I could follow a tune.

I interpreted Dad's signal as encouragement to call Mother. I grabbed a tissue and mopped my eyes and nose once more. I needed to sound normal, not blubbering, because she didn't need the burden of my pain on top of hers. Slowly, I dialed her number.

When she answered, I said, "Mom, you'll never believe what just happened."

"I bet I will," she said. I heard tears in her voice.

Puzzled at her reaction, I said, "Dad was just here in my living room. He sat in his chair across the room from me and we talked."

Through a sob she asked, "What did he say?" Not a trace of doubt permeated her words.

"He asked me to look out for you and to tell you he wanted you to be there for us because he can't. He said he was sorry."

"That's what he told me too," Mother said.

"You saw him?" I asked her. Her unexpected news was a big relief. At least I wasn't the only one seeing things this time. But it also made me cry again, and we sat on the phone weeping together.

After a moment, she blew her nose and told me what she had experienced. "I was so discouraged, I didn't want to go on living. And then, suddenly, he was here. He sat down next to me on the bed and held me." She sobbed, and I felt like I was intruding on my parents' private moment.

"He told me the same thing he said to you, that I needed to be there for all of you because he couldn't." She paused, remembering. "And he apologized for the mess he left me in. He's upset because just before we went to Newport News to see Grandpa Elsie, he had knocked all the plaster off the walls in the attic room and left a big mess. He was going to re-plaster the room and make it into a study. Now, all that junk from the walls is in the middle of the room. I have no idea what to do about it."

Mother and Dad had purchased the old Victorian and converted one side into apartments while they lived in the other. Dad finished the apartments, and they were rented out, providing some additional income. He had started the repairs on their side of the house and had completed everything but the third floor. Luckily, Mother's studio was one of the rooms he had finished. The last to be done was the one with the downed plaster. I would have to get some friends to help me put things in order for her.

She sighed. "You know it's interesting what he did in the last month of his life?" I heard her tissue brush the phone as she continued. "He went to visit everyone in the family. On that trip out to Seattle, he stopped in Chicago to see Susan and got to play with Tracy. He visited you and spent time with Blake. Then he insisted that we make that trip to Newport News to see Elsie because we hadn't been there in a while. I didn't want him to take that drive because he had been so terribly tired lately. Of course, he wouldn't let me do the driving. When we got to your Aunt Alice's, he had to lie down and take a rest. You know that's not like him at all."

Mother thought for a moment, and then said, "Hmm. He decided to get that physical. I wonder if he knew something was wrong?"

I told Mother about Dad's last visit to my house, two days before he died. I explained my feeling of dread and described the intensity of his goodbye. I said, "As he drove away, I knew that I would never see him again. I almost ran after him, but I couldn't have left Blake alone."

The unreality of it all, his death and now his visit, hit me. I said, "You know, Mom, that's a lot of love he has—to come back and help you like this."

She said. "That makes it even harder in some ways. But you're right. He does love us a lot, doesn't he?"

I said, "Yes, he does." Then I remembered how Dad had looked when his ghost appeared to me. I asked her, "Was he wearing that ratty cranberry sweater when you saw him?" She laughed for the first time since she had picked up the phone. "He was. He knows how much it annoys me. Do you have any idea how many times I tried to throw that old thing away? He always managed to rescue it."

I offered, "He did it deliberately just to make us laugh."

"You're right, Nancy," she said firmly. "It's a comfort to know he's somewhere, but the world is so empty without him. He was such a happy enthusiastic man, always ready to drop everything and go for a drive or start some new project with me. I know I'm lucky to have had a husband who cared so much and loved my company. Being without him is so hard because he was so present in my life—" Mother stopped and I heard her crying softly again.

"When we lived in Chile," I said, "and you left for home early to take that trip around the States, he talked about being apart from you. He felt like half a person when you weren't there. He told me that it was unfair of him to say it, but he hoped he would die first because he could not live without you. You'd be able to handle his death better than he could yours because you were stronger."

"I think he overestimated me," she said, scoffing. "I'm not as strong as he thought. I have to force myself to do everything, but he's right: I must get my act together." As the call ended, she said, "Thank you for being with me, Nancy. You're so much like him, it's almost like having a piece of him here."

The phone calls with Susan and my mother exhausted me. I hadn't slept much since Dad's death. Most nights, I would lie awake, staring at the ceiling. I had found that if I read sitting in the recliner until I started to doze, then I could drag myself into bed and drift off for a short time.

Falling asleep had never been a problem before. I am one of those lucky people who hit the pillow and zonk out right away, and I missed getting my mind to be quiet so I could sleep. My lack of restful sleep led me to nod off for short naps during the day, which wasn't safe with busy Blake around. He was quite observant and took my slumber as permission to get into whatever he knew he wasn't supposed to get into.

Just a day earlier, he had made stair steps out of a row of drawers to climb up on the kitchen counter and get in the sugar canister. At all times he was a serious handful. Blake was exceptionally smart, and yet he had no sense at all about danger. He climbed everything in sight just because it was there. Dad had said he was probably going to be an adventurer because he was so daring.

After the canister incident, Blake had come over to me and using his limited vocabulary he asked, "Dampa where?" Dad's last visit was recent enough that I felt his question came from some small understanding that something had changed and it involved his grandfather. I hugged him, but I could not explain to him yet that Dampa was gone, and we weren't going to get to see him again.

Blake bounced off my lap and tore across the living room and patted the chair where Dad had sat reading the animal book with him on his last visit. "Dampa where?" He asked it again as if sure that I didn't understand his question.

"I'm sorry, son, but Grandpa died and he is in heaven now. We won't get to see him any more." I had no idea how much of my explanation he could understand.

"Dampa all gone?"

"That's right, hon, he is all gone." He stormed across the room, buried his little curly head in my lap and bawled. Suddenly Blake's head flew up and I saw fear in his eyes.

"Danma all gone?"

"No, honey, Grandma is at her house. She is not all gone." The sun came out on his little face and he danced around the living room celebrating that Danma was not all gone. I got up and celebrated with him, suddenly as happy as he was that she was still with us.

I had told Blake that he would never see his grandfather again, but I didn't really know if that was true. Was it possible for my son to see him? My father the ghost seemed incongruous to me. Dad was a particularly sensible man, and although I knew he had seen ghosts during his life because he had told me so, it still seemed strange that he was now coming back in ghostly form. Life was in no way simple.

I had experienced a real conversation with my dead father and so had my mother. Even with my own abilities, my understanding of my dad's experiences, and my belief in the other side of life, this event seemed surreal. Downstairs I curled up with a blanket and a book, but I couldn't concentrate enough to understand what I was reading. I kept glancing at his chair, wondering. Was it a one-time thing? Would he ever reappear? Had I seen him for the last time in this ghostly form before he moved on to parts unknown? Or would he be back?

Chapter 4

Call Your Mom

Several months went by before I saw my father again. I continued to struggle with the loss of my best friend and the only other person I knew who had intuitive skills like those I was just coming to understand.

I was jolted out of the memory of my last view of my father alive when Blake announced, "I go fishin'!" and headed into the powder room. He slept little and possessed boundless energy, not to mention that ever-present penchant for disaster. I caught him just before he dove into the toilet again. I had to remember not to leave that door open!

I called Mother often so she wouldn't feel alone. As much as she needed the contact with me, I needed to talk to her to be certain she was all right. I had no sense that she was going to die, but I knew her grief was sometimes overwhelming and that concerned me.

The comfort of my father's existence on the other side stayed with me as I visited Mother each week with Blake in tow. The recent arrival of my second adopted son, Travis, was a wonderful distraction for both Mother and me. Sometimes she even showed signs that she was beginning to adjust to being alone.

The night after one such visit to Mom's house, Blake and Travis were both tucked in bed. Blake had finally capitulated and stopped resisting sleep. I finished the last dinner dish and turned to head for my favorite reading chair, and I ran into my father. Literally. He was as solid as I was.

He looked at me with great urgency and commanded, "Call your mother. Now." Then he disappeared.

I whirled around and grabbed the phone. My fingers picked out my mother's number, and I heard her say a distressed hello.

"What's wrong?" I demanded.

Through tears she said, "Fred was just here. I was so low. I miss him terribly. He appeared and he insisted that I 'get it together.'" I could hear her draw in a deep breath.

I said, "He was here in my kitchen too. He ordered me to call you right away. I knew something was wrong by the look in his eyes."

"He has no idea how hard this is for me," Mother said.

"I think he does know, Mom," I told her. "He comes back to help you because he understands." I paused as something strange occurred to me. "You know, I bumped into him."

"What do you mean?" she asked.

I recounted how I had rounded the corner into the living room and had run right into him. "He was as solid as he was when he was alive," I said, and laughed at the thought of what he was wearing. "He still has that raggedy sweater on."

She managed a small chuckle too. "He haunts us with it."

I thought about what was happening. "This is remarkable. He's there when you need him even now."

I could hear Mother begin to cry again, and I tried to soothe her by reminding her that Dad came back for her. She considered what I had said and then added, "I wonder if he will keep coming back or if this is just something that happens at first; you know, right after death." I had been wondering the same thing, but I had no answers.

"Who would have ever thought Dad would be a ghost," I remarked.

She thought about it. "As sensible as your father was, this seems out of character. He's not exactly the kind of person I'd expect to haunt me, although this certainly is a good haunting."

"Dad's love for you is not out of character." I said.

"I miss being hugged," she sighed. "He always hugged me."

"I miss that too," I said. "I don't think that hole will ever be filled in our lives." Good going, Nancy! I wanted to kick myself as soon as I said it. Nothing like grinding the truth in at the wrong moment.

I shifted the discussion to the latest scrape Blake had gotten into. He had put a plastic bowl in the oven and turned it on. The bowl was full of mud, a pie that he wanted to bake. Luckily I smelled a strange odor and tracked it down just as the plastic bowl started to melt.

Mom and I both laughed hard at Blake's incredible imagination. He could figure out how to work things that any other child his age would never even notice.

As we chatted, I felt a firm hand on my shoulder. I turned to see my father. He smiled, gave me a pat on the shoulder, winked, and was gone.

"He just came back," I heard myself say.

"Blake?"

"Dad," I said. "He put his hand on my shoulder and gave me a wink. You know the way he always did?"

"Yes," Mother said with a small catch in her voice, "when you had done a good job at something."

"That's right," I said. "He would always do that." I hadn't forgotten, but somehow I didn't expect him to remember it as a ghost. Was this ghost equipped with all my dad's thoughts and memories, or was it merely a shadow of him?

"You did do a good job," Mother said. "Here. Today."

I hung up the phone relieved to hear her say that I was helping, but what really struck me was the power of my father. He was capable of crossing over from death to touch us, to be there, to help.

Right after my dad's death, my shock and grief at his untimely passing left me empty of thought in a strange way. The first time he appeared to me, I couldn't think clearly enough to form questions to ask him and during those first months, I was too numb to register the greater significance of his appearances. I had always been a curious person and it wasn't like me to ignore something this big. Now, slowly, my mind was starting to process these occurrences.

Later that night I sat in my chair, my book forgotten in my lap as I took in the quiet and reviewed the memories of Dad's ghostly visits. I heard his voice, strong and clear right beside me.

"Over here, thoughts are things," he said.

Then he was sitting opposite me. *Thoughts are things.* I looked at him and said, "What does that mean?"

He considered my question and said, "Where I am, what you create in your imagination you can make real."

I wondered aloud, "If that's true, why doesn't everyone there do it?"

He said, "You need to have the right kind of energy from the living to do it. You and your mother have it. I can use that to build my image."

"When I ran into you earlier," I said, "you felt solid just like you did in life, except that you were cold."

He said, "I wanted to seem real to you so that you wouldn't be afraid of me."

"Oh yeah," I said, "I'm likely to be afraid of you. It is strange though. I mean, talking to a ghost. No offense."

His deep laugh spilled out. "I know how fond of ghosts you are. You always hated Halloween." I joined in his laughter.

"Oh, that was real nice," I chided, "the way you died on Halloween. Now I seriously hate it."

His face showed regret. "That was a mistake. I went too soon."

Sadness filled the air around us. I looked into his eyes and saw his pain at being separated from us. He was suffering as much as Mother and I were. He lowered his head so I wouldn't continue to see his pain, then he disappeared from view, but I still heard what sounded like his breathing. Dad cleared his throat. I knew he was still sitting across the room from me, invisible but there.

"How come I can hear you but not see you right now?" I asked.

"It takes too much energy to create the appearance of a physical body for long. This is easier," he answered. But I suspected the real reason was that he didn't want me to see his face and his sadness.

I said, "Makes me feel like I'm crazy or imagining all this."

"You were born with second sight, Nancy. You know that, and you're learning to handle that awareness of what your skill is. Now, you'll learn about the other things you can do with your mind."

Amazing, even now he was still my best and favorite teacher. I so wanted to prolong my conversation with him, so I asked him something I had wondered about since his death.

"Charles Smack came to your funeral." I couldn't see Dad, but I had a feeling he was smiling. "He brought with him the men you had saved from death at the hands of the Klan. What were you thinking putting yourself in danger like that?"

After a moment, he answered my question, his tone serious. "I just knew I had to stop them from killing that night. And I had a way to do it. People in that part of the country couldn't afford more than one pair of shoes. I saw those white men—and their shoes—every day. I worked alongside them. I recognized all the men under the hoods by the shoes on their feet and called every one of them by name. That scared them, and I don't think they knew how I did it, but it was enough to stop them."

I felt him leave suddenly as if the breath were sucked out of my chest. I cried hard for a while. Mother was right: Earlier on the phone she had said his visits made the grief stronger, but it was also worth it to know he still watched over us.

To counter my sorrow I reached into the past and pulled out a sunlit memory. I was holding tools for Dad while he worked on the washing machine. We lived in Chillán, Chile, and there were no repairmen, so my Dad's magic with machinery came in handy. His tall frame was wound around the machine as he carefully dismantled it and lined up each piece on a clean old towel in the order in which he had removed them. I was around eight then and my favorite thing was to hang around and hand Dad tools so that I could spend the time talking with him.

"How did you meet Mommy," I asked.

He looked around the machine at me with a twinkle in his eye. "You've heard that a hundred times." Back he went to dismantling the washing machine.

"I know that. I just like to hear you tell it."

"Well, I was a student at the University of Delaware in the Ag department. They wanted some of the students to do an assembly at Harrington High School on majoring in agriculture at the university. I volunteered to go."

"Why'd you volunteer to go?"

"Well, it got me out of class and barn duty that day, and I had heard there were some pretty, single teachers at that school." He leaned around the machine and winked. "I found out I had heard right too," he laughed.

"Anyway, I'm up on this platform in front of the whole student body, and I see this lovely young woman sitting below, off to my right." He stopped working as he always did when he got to this part. "She was beautiful, and I decided I was going to have to meet her that day."

I giggled with anticipation.

"After the assembly was over my friend George Vappa, a teacher there, invited us to lunch in the cafeteria. Well, I was always hungry so I was happy to go along. When we got to the cafeteria, there she was again, the beautiful young woman. She had lunch duty that day, and I convinced George to introduce us." He laughed as he remembered the next part. "George warned me she was from New York City and was probably way too smart for the likes of me, but he introduced us anyway."

He sat up with a black, soggy sock in his hand and said, "Here's our culprit, one of my socks. Now all I have to figure out is what that sock was doing in the drain. It shouldn't have been able to get in there." Back to work he went.

He busied himself with the machine until my plaintive "Daddy, stop teasing me!" brought another chuckle out of him.

"So I started talking to this goddess, and I found out she was kind of shy and she was real nice. I asked her if she liked to dance. She said she did, very much, so I asked her to the dance that Saturday at the college. She looked a little upset and said she'd love to come but she didn't have a way to get there. I asked her if she would mind riding up with George Vappa and his girlfriend. He was driving to the dance and I was sure he wouldn't mind bringing her up too. And that is how I met your mother." He sat up and wiped the oil off his hands. All the parts had disappeared back into the machine in a matter of minutes. He was magical at fixing things.

He waved me off. "Now, go pester your mom for a while. I have things to do up on the ladder, and I can't be distracted when I'm fixing the roof." Our roof was made of tile, and the cats walked across it, knocking the tiles out of position. Sometimes, when they got into fights they knocked the tiles off completely and they would smash on impact with the ground. That's what had happened the night before, and Dad had to fix it before the rain came in through the new hole in the roof.

I heaved a big sigh and flounced off. I knew I wasn't supposed to bother him when he was up on a ladder.

Chapter 5

The Man in the Garden

When my Father appeared to me, he seemed as solid as he did in life, yet cold to the touch. The air in the room around him was frigid as well. Sometimes it got so cold I had to turn the thermostat up. I had felt that coldness around other ghosts too. As a child I had seen ghosts, but they were people I didn't know and I was afraid of them, so I tried to ignore them. I refused to deal with the reality of what their presence meant. Seeing the ghost of my father felt completely different. He was the same as he had been when he was alive—same personality, same sense of humor. His presence seemed so natural. Where I had, in most cases, rejected the appearance of the other ghosts who had contacted me, I welcomed Dad.

One encounter with a ghost happened the time I was in the infirmary at my boarding school in Santiago, Chile. While flying down a hill on my roller skates using my coat as a wind sail, I crashed head first into the road, spraining both arms and giving myself a serious whack on the head. As a consequence, I was stuck in the infirmary with nothing to do. The staff would bring me books, and I'd polish them off in a matter of hours and then sit there feeling sorry for myself. I was even sorry to miss classes because at least that was something to do, but until the dizziness from the bang on my head stopped, the doctor wouldn't let me go back to class. What would I do there anyway? I couldn't use my hands at all because both arms hurt so much.

As I moped in my bed on one particularly spectacular morning, the sun streamed into the little sundial garden I could see from my window. I climbed up on a chair to look out the high opening and smell the fresh air. I was surprised to see an old man in the garden feeding the pigeons. Few men were allowed on the property of this all-girls school.

"Hello, Nancy. How are you feeling?" asked the man, tipping his hat like some fancy gentleman from olden times. I had never met this man before, so how did he know my name?

As if he could read my mind he said, "I know Harriet." Harriet was my mother's name. The man seemed to sense my mistrust and chuckled to himself. "You're a lot like her, you know. She was always up to mischief and getting herself banged up. I'll bet if she had had roller skates, she would have tried the same trick that you did," he said, smiling up at me. "Like the time she ate the caterpillar! I don't think I ever laughed so hard as I did that day."

How on earth did he know about that? Who was this guy who knew Mother? I knew about her eating the caterpillar because I was her daughter and she had told me the story. But how did he know?

I was not comfortable with this stranger. I glared at him, and I was offended when he laughed at me!

"I apologize," he said, "but your scowl so resembles Harriet's that I couldn't help myself."

Just then Nursey came to the door to check on me. "I heard a man's voice," she said sternly. "Who are you talking to?" As this was a girls' school, any male voice raised suspicion.

"That guy in the garden feeding the pigeons," I answered, pointing out the window at him.

Nursey dragged another chair over, as she was quite short, and climbed up to look.

"There's no one out there. But I heard a man's voice," she said impatiently.

The man bowed and tipped his hat, then he went back to feeding the pigeons.

"He's right there," I said. "See how he's throwing the food to the birds."

Nursey stiffened and then she screamed like a madwoman, ran out into the hall, and locked me in my room. I stood on my chair staring after her in shock.

The man in the garden was still watching me. I said to him, "Nursey just went crazy. She ran out and locked me in the room. The bathroom is on the other side of that door. What am I going to do now?" Her wild exit from my room frightened me. Why was she so scared?

Again it seemed that the old man could deduce what I was thinking, even though I did not say anything out loud. He explained, "She's frightened of what she does not understand."

"What are you talking about?" I asked, peeved.

"Nursey couldn't see me, but she could tell I was there. She could see only seeds being thrown to the pigeons—from nowhere. That was enough to send her off screaming. You see, I am your mother's grandfather—your great-grandfather—and your Nursey friend apparently is afraid of ghosts." He had a big grin on his face as if this were the greatest fun.

"I'm afraid of ghosts too!" I said. Only now did I realize that I could see the garden through his faintly transparent shape.

"Are you afraid of me?" he asked.

"No, I'm not. That's kind of strange because I don't know you."

"Yes, but I'm still a relative, a distant relative," he laughed so hard he had to bend over, and his hat fell off. We laughed together, and then we had a good conversation about what his life had been like and the voyages he had sailed back and forth between New York and France, braving huge storms to transport goods. I remembered Mother talking about how much fun it had been to hear his stories about his voyages, and now I was getting to hear them firsthand.

My great-grandfather's ghost gradually disappeared in front of my eyes. I sat down on my bed after he was gone. I knew now that I was going to have to rethink this ghost stuff because he wasn't scary at all. In fact, he made me feel less lonely. Maybe he would visit me again because it really was lonely in the infirmary.

When I got up to go get Nursey—I hadn't had breakfast yet—I discovered that my door was still locked. By lunchtime, I was just plain angry. There was a phone in the room, and I knew the headmistress's apartment number, so I dialed it and asked her to come let me out and could I please have something to eat as I hadn't eaten all day.

Miss Mason lived just above the infirmary so she arrived quickly, and I heard her questioning Nursey outside the door. Then the key turned in my door and I made a run for the facilities. When I came out, I found a lunch tray and Miss Mason sitting in my room, waiting to talk to me. How on earth was I going to explain the ghost to her? I hoped she didn't know about him, but I could tell by the way she studied me that she did know. She always knew what children were up to.

We had quite an interesting talk about ghosts. Miss Mason had seen several in castles she had visited, and she believed that they were real, which was a surprise to me. She wanted to know all about the ghost in the garden. She let Nursey go to lunch and take a rest, while she and I sat eating together discussing ghosts. I did not think that adults believed in such things, but I was relieved to know that Miss Mason, whom I knew to be a smart, sensible lady, did believe in ghosts, and that made it a little less confusing for me.

On my next vacation home, I carefully questioned Mother about her grandfather. What was he like and, most important, what did he look like? "Oh, I'll show you," she said as she reached for her family photo album.

She pointed out his photo and talked to me about how wonderful he was and how much he loved her and her brother Edward. Of course, it was a photo of the man in the sundial garden. Until that very moment I could pretend to myself that what I had seen was not real. The photo shut down that fantasy. The man in the garden was much younger than the man in the photo, but it was still clear that this was in fact the fellow—the ghost—I had visited with.

"Why are you asking about him?" Mother asked.

"Remember when I was in the infirmary at school after I hurt my wrists? I had a visitor in the garden outside my room." I tapped the edge of the photo. "It was him, Mom. He even knew about you eating the caterpillar! It was really him. He says that when I scowl, I look just like you."

Mother stared at me. She was shocked. Then she reached into her pocket for a hanky to dab at tears in her eyes.

"I'm sorry, Mom," I said as I patted her hands. "I didn't mean to upset you."

"It's all right. He was my favorite grandfather and so much fun to be with. When Edward and I were stuck in bed with some childhood illness or other, he would sneak into our rooms and bring us toys he had made, or he would just chat with us until our mother shooed him out. After all these years, I still miss him, but I am glad that you told me this story." She patted my hands, and then left the room.

What good did it do for this ghost to come back if it made Mother so sad? Throughout my life and my career this question has haunted me. My knowing that there are ghosts is one thing, but should I really tell anyone that they are there? Does it help people to know that their loved ones are still around, in a different form, or should I not say anything about it?

In the days that followed my talk with my mother, I saw that she seemed very happy. She asked me a lot of questions about the visit from my great-grandfather, and I could tell she was trying to be sure that his appearance was not a figment of my creative mind. Gradually, my answers to her questions convinced her that I was not making it up. I knew too many things that I could not have figured out on my own. I could tell that she appreciated knowing he still existed and was able to offer me comfort when I was sick, just as he did with Mother and Uncle Edward when they were little. "That is so like him," she said.

The paranormal events of my life have led me to conclude that it's a good thing for people to know that the spirits of those they loved are there and still care about them, even though they have passed on to another type of reality. The links with those we love do not break when life stops. That information has allowed me over the years to help many grieving people make peace with their losses and understand that there is a lot more to life than any of us know.

Having my father's ghost visit with me was very different from meeting the ghost of my great-grandfather because I had never known him. But Dad's visits, in some ways comforting, also brought back the loss I felt with his death. He could no longer give me a warm bear hug; we couldn't take off for a drive together so he could stop to check out the progress of the farmers' crops in the fields we passed. Sometimes I wondered if it would be better if I couldn't see him at all, but I knew that his visits comforted both Mother and me. It showed us how much he loved us, that even though he was dead, he kept coming back to comfort us. It emphasized for me just how remarkable and loving a man he was in life—and now in death. I came to treasure those visits and to see them as the new normal for me.

I was getting used to hearing Dad's occasional comments inside my head. I didn't tell people about it because I didn't want to seem nuts, or worse yet, so stricken with grief that I had lost touch with reality. In my heart I was certain it wasn't my grief that caused him to appear. I felt that, as always, Dad was giving me important lessons in life. Or in this case, death. On his next visit, I asked him, "Where are you when you aren't here?"

Dad was sitting across the living room in his favorite chair when he looked at me with a smile and said, "I wondered when you would get around to asking that." He thought for a bit. "I think the best way to explain it is that I am a part of the Light of Life now."

I was a little afraid to push too hard with questions because now I knew that it took a tremendous amount of energy for him to manifest, and I did not want him to disappear. But his answer wasn't exactly satisfactory. Light of Life? I said, "What does that mean?"

I could see Dad mulling over what to say, as if he had to come up with terms a living person could grasp. Finally, he said, "Every soul is made up of light that derives its existence from what people would generally refer to as God. A soul, when it enters a body at the time of that being's birth, changes form and accommodates the limitations of the particular body it inhabits. For example, dogs can't talk, so a soul within a dog must adjust to that lack of verbal communication. The soul inhabits that body until the term of that body's life ends—or some unpleasant event interrupts the natural life span of that body. Then the soul transfers back to its original form in the Light of Life. Does that help?"

"Well. Yes. Somewhat," I stammered. "So you are in light form when you're not here. Can you hear and communicate in that form?" I asked.

"Oh, yes," he said, "I am in constant communication with the Light of Life itself as well as the other, more advanced souls who are teaching me how to grow."

He added that he can hear and follow what is going on with the people he loves, like Mother and his children and grandchildren.

"I can also communicate with family members who died before me," he said. "We're all linked by our love and the Light of Life.

"I know it must sound strange to you," he went on, "but it is very real. I feel different from when I was alive on your plane, because I no longer have a body to deal with. That part of it is freeing. As I explained to you before, thoughts are things, and that concept would not work if I were still in a body. In this form—as light—I can be anywhere that I am needed, sometimes in more than one place at a time, just by thinking about it."

I thought about the implications of what he was saying. "So, for you, mind travel is a reality?"

He considered my question and said, "What's hardest to understand— at least I think it is—is that time is not linear. Everything exists together, at once. That mystery will take me a while to fully understand. Being in this light doesn't automatically mean I know everything. I'm still learning on this plane too. Sorry, I can't explain better. . . ."

He slowly vanished.

Chapter 6
Double Feature

I was busy with another Blake mess in the kitchen when I felt the extreme cold draft that signaled Dad was about to make an appearance. I turned around to see him laughing at me with a twinkle in his eye. I felt surrounded by his love.

"You're so domestic, Nance," he said. "It's not you."

"It is now," I returned. "It might not seem in character for me, but I actually enjoy bringing order to chaos."

He stood there for a moment. "I want you to know I appreciate what you do for your mother. It's been a hard three years for her. She's better, but it has been terribly lonely for her. You and Blake and Travis have become her life since I've been gone."

I loved that Dad could know both my children, even though he had not met Travis in life. We had been on the waiting list for Travis when Dad died. He was just two-and-a-half months old when he arrived in our home, and in that short time since his birth, he had been moved around many times. He refused to eat and didn't react to anything at first. I carried him around in a nursing mother sling so that he could start to bond with me. The only time I put him down was when I was cooking. Then Blake would sit beside the little day crib and pat his brother's tummy nonstop so Travis would not feel so alone.

One time Travis giggled and smiled at his brother's silly rubber ducky dance. Blake squealed in delight, thrilled that this little person had smiled at him.

"Mom, he laughin' funny!"

I ran in from the kitchen to find Blake dancing around like a nut, and Travis giggling away at him. Breakthrough! I was so relieved that night when Travis took his bottle for the first time, and with enthusiasm. He was due to go to the hospital the following day if we could not get him to eat. I gave Blake extra dessert that night for helping his little brother to feel comfortable with us. Travis's deep, elated baby-giggle was here to stay, and Blake delighted in doing crazy things so he could hear it.

So I guess I *was* domestic after all.

Standing there in the kitchen, Dad said, "You have a daughter yet to come, and she will be quite a handful." He smiled. "Like you."

The idea of adopting again had crossed my mind. "Oh, great," I sighed, "another Blake."

"No," he said seriously, "she won't have the energy he has. She is more like you. Actually, she'll be more like your mother." He smiled again as he started to fade out. "By the way," he said, half there, half not, "she will be born to you." And he was gone.

I stared in shock at the place where he had stood. After experiencing six pregnancies that resulted in six miscarriages, I believed that what he said was unlikely at best. I carried in my heart the wrenching loss of each little baby that did not survive. My adopted sons healed a lot of the pain, and more than anything I loved being their mom.

The doctors had never been able to tell me what caused my babies to die, and I had resigned myself to never giving birth to a child. After the boys' adoptions, I thought to myself, "Who needs labor pains anyway!" I immersed myself in the fun that accompanied the arrival of each of my boys and loved them fully as I watched them grow, walk, talk, and become their own special selves. They were my miracles and I was happy—at peace with my lost babies. Yet, I recently saw a pair of lovely blue eyes in my dreams, and I knew it was a little girl. I had dreams of the boys' eyes before I held my sons in my arms. When I first met them, I recognized them instantly by their eyes. Could it be possible that the eyes I was dreaming about now belonged to the daughter Dad predicted? I forced myself to shut that out as an unrealistic expectation that would only leave me heart-broken again.

The phone rang. I grabbed it.

It was my sister Susan calling from Schaumburg, Illinois. She was breathless. "He was just here!" she said.

This was an event: the first time she had seen our dad since his death.

"He was here too," I told her.

"You mean just now?" she asked.

"Yep, just here."

"How can he be in two places at once?" she said. "I mean, there's even a time difference between us."

I shrugged. "He tried to explain it to me. It's that 'thoughts are things' stuff he's talked about to me. He can visualize himself in two places and boom, he's there."

"I guess," Susan said and then paused. "Nancy, he said you were going to have a daughter."

"He told me that too! He said she would be born to me—fat chance of that. All I ever do is miscarry."

"I know," said Susan. "Wouldn't it be wonderful though!"

I thought about it, and hesitated. "I don't know. The boys might feel left out because they're adopted."

"Well, if I were you," Susan stated, "I'd prepare to get pregnant and stay pregnant this time."

I found an excuse to cut off the call, not wanting to open up those wounds. I distracted myself by preparing dinner. From the backyard, I heard Travis's familiar call, "Mom, I need you now!" At nearly four, Travis was an able watchdog who notified me about disasters Blake created.

I ran to the back door to check on the boys. The latest crisis was the normal story: "Blake's not sharing. He's taking my trucks!"

Blake was 17 months older than Travis and used his size and aggres-siveness to take advantage of his younger brother. I tried to warn Blake that Travis was growing rapidly and one day would be big enough to defend himself.

After playing peacemaker, I ran back inside to finish cooking dinner. I wondered, did Dad know what he knew just because he was on the other side? When he was alive, he had known things about the future, and I was like him in that way. He always seemed to be tuned in on what would happen next, and I used to think it was because he knew so much about agriculture and things in general. Now that I was able to have similar insights, I knew it was something more. It felt a little strange when I would know something and have no logical reason to know it.

Inside, I too had felt that a baby girl was coming to me; I had always felt I would have a daughter. I dreamt about her when I was small and even picked out just the right name, Heidi, the title of my favorite book when I was nine. That was when I first had dreams about her blue eyes. Was it just a coincidence that I had started to dream about them again?

It seemed like Dad had played a joke on Susan and me today, appearing to both of us at the same time. I wondered if he had appeared to Mother too? I picked up the receiver and tried to think of a casual way to ask Mother if my father's ghost had visited her today.

"Hi, Ma," I said. That was good for starters.

"Hello yourself," she responded pleasantly.

We exchanged the usual catching-up conversation—her job at the radio station in Dover, Blake's latest prank.

Then Mother said out of nowhere, "I hear him every now and then."

The way she said it—*him*—I knew who she meant. "Oh." I couldn't think of what else to say.

"I'll be busy, and then all of a sudden I hear his whistle and his steps on the front porch. Then his key turns in the lock. I think to myself that I had better hurry and make our lunch." She cleared her throat. "Then the noise stops and I remember he's gone."

"He showed up here tonight and at Susan's at the same time," I said.

"Hmm. Who'd have thought he could do that," she said.

"Ma, he wanted me to know I'm going to have a daughter." I waited a beat. "A daughter born to me."

Silence hung for a moment, then my mother whispered, "Oh, Nancy." I heard the apprehension in her voice. I wasn't sure if she was worried about my spirits if a pregnancy didn't happen or my health if it did.

"How can he know that?" she asked. "Did he say when?"

"Just, soon." The weight of her concern hung between us, so I tried to lighten up the mood. "He said she'll be a handful because she's like you and me mixed together."

"Oh brother!" said Mom. "That *will* be a handful."

We laughed and talked on about the boys. As usual Blake's latest prank filled us with life and laughter. Travis was at the moment tugging on my shirt, trying to get my attention. I put my arm around him and he snuggled up to me while I went on talking with Mother. I brushed the sweaty curls back from Travis's forehead.

"Travis is worried about Blake," I told Mother.

She chuckled, "He's not the only one."

"He says he's sure Blake doesn't mean to be bad. It's just an accident." I added, "Or in his case, a series of accidents. I'd better find out what's going on. Bye now, Mom."

And off I went with Travis to find out more about Blake's misadventure.

When my husband and I adopted our sons, we never expected to find ourselves in an accidental experiment. Each of the children was a first-born child with first-born characteristics. Each in his own way was a leader with a strong personality. The strangest thing to me was that they each had psychic gifts. Don't misunderstand me—many people have psychic gifts, so that wasn't odd; what was odd was the extent of their abilities.

Early on, Blake showed a talent for finding anything we lost. His abilities extended to uncovering things we tried to hide from him, like gifts and candy. When something disappeared, the family came to me first; they went to Blake next. His method of searching was more destructive than mine because he tossed stuff every which way, but he would find what was missing. The more he helped people look for missing articles, the more his accuracy improved. That was the way it worked for me too. This confirmed what I believed—that this was a skill that one could develop if one had the natural talent.

Travis, I discovered, had healing skills. A little girl, only three years old, who lived in our neighborhood had been diagnosed with cancer. Travis was hanging around listening as I talked with her mother. He overheard her mother talk about how lonely the child was because she wasn't allowed to play outside.

"I can come over and play with her, can't I, Mom?" Travis offered.

"Yes, you can if you would like to," I said.

"You let me know when, Mom," he said as he ran off to play.

He visited the little girl that afternoon when she got up from her nap. Her mother had warned me that she was quite weak, but her spirits were good. As we crossed the street to her house, I warned Travis: "Her mom says she doesn't have much energy, but she's a brave little girl, and I am proud of you for volunteering to play with her. She is very sick, and if that makes you too uncomfortable, we won't stay long. We won't be able to stay too long anyway, as she tires easily."

"Okay, Mom," he said thoughtfully. "She probably likes dolls. Guess I'll have to play with those."

"I don't know, Travis. If I remember right, she likes to play ball. But she has to stay inside."

Travis sat on the floor playing ball with the little girl. He would gently throw it into her lap, and she would giggle and toss it back. As the game continued, she slid closer and closer to Travis, smiling and laughing and clearly having a good time. Toward the end of their playtime, she was snuggled right up against him sound asleep. We tiptoed out so the child could rest.

Back home, Travis and I sat at the table in the kitchen eating cookies. Blake was at a friend's house, so we had the place to ourselves. Travis was quiet and had a serious look on his face. "Mom, I have a bad feeling that little girl is not going to be all right. What do you think?"

"I hate to say it," I told him, "but I agree with you. That is so sad, but at least you brightened her day."

He munched on his cookies quietly for a bit and then said, "She's not bad for a girl. I'm tired. Is it okay if I take a nap?"

"Of course. Go right ahead." I was in shock. He hadn't taken a nap in quite some time. Maybe this was too much for him.

The next morning my neighbor called and reported, "She's dancing around the living room and says she doesn't hurt much today. She told me that nice boy took her pain away, and she wanted me to thank him. I hate to ask this, but could he come and visit her again?"

"I'll ask him and see how he feels," I replied. "I'll let you know."

I began to suspect why Travis was so tired: Could it be that he had healing abilities? It would explain his fatigue and the fact that she was relatively pain free after being with him. But I didn't want him to be exhausted, so if he chose to go again, we would stay a shorter time.

We went for two more visits. Each time Travis was more tired, but the little girl felt better. I wouldn't let him go after that because it was too much for him. I had healing skills too, so instead I visited her, holding her in my lap and talking to her, so that I could transfer energy into her. I wish I could say that she survived, but she did not. During the last months of her life, however, she was relatively pain free. Her mother told me the doctors were mystified by that. They said that with her illness, the pain usually increased toward the end.

When I told the boys she had died, they were both upset.

"I thought only old people died," said Blake.

"I thought we helped her," added Travis.

"We did help her," I told them. "Her mother said she hardly had any pain after you started visiting, and that's unusual."

"I don't think it's fair for little kids to die," said Blake.

Travis said, "I don't think it is either. She was my friend."

We spent the afternoon in the park to keep their minds busy with other things.

The boys and I had talked before about what death was, but it was difficult to gauge how much they actually understood at their young ages. And despite living their short lives so far in a house where I communed with my dead father, this was the first time my boys were conscious of the death of someone they knew.

Chapter 7
Death by VW

I played a game called Ouija with a friend. She was waiting to be notified by her adoption agency that they had secured a baby for her. I knew how long that wait was, and so I invited her over to help pass the time, and she brought the Ouija board with her. I played the game, and it turned out to be very interesting, so the next day I bought a Ouija for myself. That was a terrible mistake.

In the days that followed, strange things happened. First, the contents of an oversized glass bottle of grape juice went airborne in my kitchen. The top flew off and a geyser of grape juice shot almost to the ceiling, and then poured all over the kitchen floor. Somehow the bottle didn't break.

My husband and I mopped up the lake of juice in silence; I was too frightened by the incident to talk about it. I thanked goodness that the boys hadn't been awake to see it happen. Blake would likely have done his best to duplicate the juice fountain with results that would have surpassed those of the actual event.

Three days later, my husband was off running errands with Blake and Travis in tow, while I packed my dance bag and headed to ballet class in my 1960s Volkswagen "Beetle." As I made a left turn out of the housing plan, my car took off as if possessed, with a steering wheel and gear shift that refused to respond. My attempts to slam on the brakes failed to even slow the car. I tried to turn off the ignition, but nothing worked. I was on a collision course with a telephone pole.

On instinct I prayed for help and braced for impact. In that split second I felt strong, ice-cold hands close over mine. The added strength helped me to turn the car at the last minute. The Beetle stopped right up against the side of the pole. I was shaking all over and staring at my hands. The unseen force had grabbed me so hard that the backs of them hurt. I didn't care. I knew it was my father who had come to my aid, who had in fact saved my life. I knew for sure it was him because I recognized the feel of his grasp. I rubbed my hands and stared at the phone pole as if it were going to kill me still. How on earth was my father able to save me?

A woman from the neighborhood ran over. "Are you all right?" she asked.

I nodded and rolled down the window.

"Are you sure?" she asked, and I could see that she too was trembling. "You almost hit that pole!"

"The wheel wouldn't turn," I tried feebly to explain. "I couldn't get the car to stop."

"Man," she said, "I'd take that car to the shop. You could have been killed!"

All I could do was nod and give a heartfelt prayer of thanks. My hands felt like chunks of ice, and I massaged them to get the feeling back.

"Why don't I give you a ride back to your house?" the woman offered.

"Thanks. That would help."

I couldn't stop shaking or shivering—I wasn't sure which it was. I locked up the bug and climbed into the neighbor's car.

Back home I called the service department at the car dealership and tried to describe what had happened. The service rep advised, "Bring it over here right away, and we'll check it out."

I changed out of my leotard and hiked back to the car. I stared for a while, afraid to get back in. I heard my father's voice in my ear: "It's okay. It won't happen again."

I climbed in reluctantly and tried to shut down my fear by focusing on my trust in Dad. After a few seconds, my hand was steady enough to start up the bug, and I drove to the dealership with no more incidents.

An hour later, the mechanic tracked me down in the waiting room. "I can't find a thing wrong," he told me. "Steering mechanism is fine. Brakes are fine. I oiled her all up for you so she'll run like a top. If it happens again bring her back in. As far as I can tell there's nothin' wrong with this car." The mechanic delivered his report as he tried not to look at me with that "she's crazy" look.

I drove back home in confusion. The car had behaved as if it had a mind of its own—a mind bent on crashing me into the pole.

Suddenly, my father appeared beside me in the passenger seat of the VW. "Get rid of that Ouija board," he said in a grim tone. "It has attracted some negative things to you. You have a lot of psychic ability, and that makes you interesting to the wrong kind of entity."

Great! Now I had to deal with negative entities—whatever they were. Well, that darn game was going into the trash tonight! Keeping my eyes on the road, I glanced peripherally at my father's ghost. He looked completely normal sitting there with his long legs tucked up in the car's small interior, so as not to hit his knees on the dashboard. He wasn't see-through at all. He was just as solid as I was, except that the whole right side of me was freezing! These opportunities were rare and I always had questions prepared, just in case.

"Were you psychic too, Dad?" I asked. "Is that how you used to know what was going to happen in the future?"

He thought about it. "Yes, I was, but I had no idea to what extent until after I died. I knew that you had inherited whatever ability I had when you were little, because you talked about all kinds of things you had no logical way of knowing about."

There were times, like now, that I didn't want to hear such things. "I don't want to be psychic," I told him. "Psychics are weird and most of them are frauds." I knew I shouldn't complain, but the latest events had been too much for me. There was Dad right beside me, but he was a ghost and I couldn't just reach over and touch him because he might disappear. I was always mindful of the effort needed for him to do this, and I didn't want him to leave because I was scared of all of this and he always made me feel safe.

"It's not something you have a lot of choice about," he told me. "You will use it with honesty to help people. It's who you are. You can do this, Nance. It's what you are here to do." His voice faded and he disappeared as quickly as he had appeared.

I grumbled to myself, "I don't want to spend my life talking to ghosts. I mean, I don't mind my dad, but other ones? Forget it. I want a normal life."

At home, the first thing I did was to take the Ouija board out back and smash it to pieces with a hammer. I dumped the pieces in the garbage. "Some game!" I said to the trash can. I stomped back inside to return to my normal life. That illusion lasted about 10 seconds when an insistent rapping started in the kitchen wall. The garbage can was on the other side of that wall, and the pounding would not stop.

My husband and young sons walked in with groceries.

"What's banging, Mom?" Blake asked.

"I guess it's the pipes," I said.

My husband's eyebrows shot up as he walked past the wall and realized where the noise was coming from. We stared at the wall as it continued to bang, both of us knowing that there weren't any pipes in that section of wall.

"This is right up there with the grape juice fountain," I said. He nodded.

I told him what happened with the car and how my dad saved me.

"This has got to stop," said my husband.

"I know," I replied. "Dad told me to get rid of the Ouija, so I did." I shook my head in disgust. "I broke it up with the hammer and threw it in the garbage, and then the knocks started."

"Maybe something's mad at you for what you did," my husband said, half in jest.

"Well it's gone," I stated, "and I'll never get another one. No more strange stuff. Normality please!"

The rapping stopped. The sudden silence that followed my plea was as jarring as the din had been.

My husband and I looked at each other and then unloaded the groceries without exchanging a word.

I kept a close watch on Blake and Travis, worried that the next odd event might harm them in some way. They were all tucked in for the night when the knocking started again. It kept on for four hours while I pretended not to hear it. My husband retreated to his basement office. At last I prayed and asked God to help us and get this bad stuff out of our lives. As soon as I asked Him for help, the knocking ceased. My husband came upstairs and asked me what I had done to stop the noise.

"I prayed and asked God to make it stop."

"Well," he said, "keep praying. That noise is enough to drive anybody completely batty." He trudged back downstairs.

I tried to read my book as I continued to pray that we be left in peace. In the welcome silence I faced the fact that my mind was now open in a way I wasn't sure I liked. My intuition had been there all my life, but I used to be able to shove it onto the back burner when I didn't want to be troubled by it. Now that intuition barreled into my mind all the time—tidbits of information about whatever I happened to be wondering about. I knew it was psychic ability, but I wasn't sure I liked it or wanted anything to do with it. My father's appearances seemed to be connected to this growth in my abilities, but I didn't understand exactly how. I just wanted my life to be normal. I chuckled to myself. I sounded like a stuck record.

After the incident with the Ouija board and its consequences, I decided to start mentioning to people when I would get impressions about them. This caused an unexpected problem as a steady stream of friends—and later strangers—stopped by and wouldn't go home because they wanted to ask me questions all night. Finally, I set up office hours so that I could get some rest and take care of the kids. That's the odd, natural way in which my career as a psychic got started.

As time went on and I learned more about my abilities, I started to give a seminar at the local community college. During a demonstration of psychometry a gentleman handed me a ring. When I hold an object I can "read" its history—who owned that object, experiences that person had while he or she possessed it, even how a long-ago owner felt at a particular time. I sensed right away that this ring had been given to him by someone else, obviously to test me. I started the reading by looking right at the gentleman who actually owned the ring instead of the man who had handed it to me, and I began to speak about a new job that he was going to start shortly. He bolted to his feet in great nervousness and asked me to stop talking. I learned afterward that he was about to become the head of the Delaware State Police, but the news hadn't been made public yet.

For the next nine weeks, this man, Colonel Irvin Smith, called me nearly daily as he tried to convince me to assist with police work. I didn't believe I would be effective at something like that, but finally I gave in just to get him to stop calling me.

That started what would become a distinguished career as a psychic detective, working 780 missing persons and murder cases at the time of this writing, and providing information to the police that proved to be correct 90 percent of the time.

In the beginning, working with the police was nerve-wracking. I worried I would make mistakes, especially collaborating with those I called the "masters of the glare"—officers who felt that I had been forced upon them and refused to accept the information I provided about investigations. I think they felt uneasy about how accurate I could possibly be since I had not been trained in formal police procedure. On one case I got into an argument with a few of them about the cause of death: I disagreed with the medical examiner's report. When my assessment turned out to be correct, they were shocked and fired those glares at me. One look from those police officers, and I wanted to run away.

At first, it was hard for me to tolerate the cases. Murder is humanity at its worst. Only another person like me can fully understand the difficulty of my position when I work on these cases. To study or "range" a murder, I send my mind outward. It operates like a powerful antenna that picks up extraneous bits of information and images from the environment and from people around me. I have to get incredibly close to the victim's memories of the moment of death. Once my brain hooks into a murder, I can let the rest of the world fall away from me. I never know what to expect when I do this.

To work a criminal case, I must focus on the most horrible event in the victim's life: his or her murder or physical assault. A series of images of what happened to the person flows through my mind. It's like watching a movie made by the worst editor in the world. The sound track, when there is one, is barely audible, and through the mumbles I might catch the occasional clear word. I also feel physical sensations; sometimes I even feel as if I am the one attacked. The murder usually unfolds in short sequences that are not always in chronological order. I have to scramble through the images to make sense out of a senseless act and get detailed information that can help the police solve the case.

While I search through hideous images, I have to work hard to keep my emotional distance from the horror of the victim's death. Otherwise, I could never arrive at detailed information. It is the worst possible situation for a sensitive, caring person—experiencing a brutal murder, and then having to invoke analytic and critical thinking processes that no one in those circumstances would ever be able to muster. It truly is not surprising that police work is something not all psychics can do. In fact, many who attempt it burn out fast.

Despite the horrendous nature of the work, I turned out to be good at it. I thought I would fail fast, and then the well-meaning Col. Smith would leave me alone. Instead, I was forced to deal with this discovery: Not only was I able to get detail that helped the police to catch killers, I liked being instrumental in putting away bad guys so they couldn't hurt anyone else. I enjoyed shocking and surprising those cops who had started out treating me in a patronizing way. I got used to their little tricks, like mixing photos of their fellow officers with the lineup photos they showed me. When I spotted such a ringer, I would make a point of going into details about the officer's life—things he would not want his fellow cops to know about. In short order photos would get snatched back by detectives who were standing behind the glass to stop me from divulging their secrets. In time, they ended up realizing they had a new, amazingly effective tool.

Chapter 8

Rose's Story

In 1954 my family was traveling in southern Chile in an area where many families lived who had fled the war in Europe a decade or more earlier. My parents explained to us that a large percentage of these people were Jewish, and they had left their homes to stay alive. Another group of expatriates consisted of former German army officers, some of them SS. Many of these people escaped Germany and sought refuge in South America when their army was defeated and Hitler took his own life. Quite a few of these men were hunted down over time and brought to justice, and every now and then a capture would be reported in the newspapers. I remembered reading articles about the horrible things the SS officers did in the death camps of Europe.

At age eight I worried that while in Chile we might meet former SS men and they might do terrible things to us, but Dad assured me that they would seem very ordinary now, and they would not hurt anyone as they were in hiding. That helped, but it still frightened me that these scary people were living in the area we planned to visit.

Our destination on a gorgeous summer day was a place built by these European transplants to look like a German village, as many of them came from different parts of Germany and Austria. It seemed odd to me that the Jewish expatriates were living near officers of the German army and particularly the SS.

I said to my dad, "How can they live right next to each other and get along?"

"Not everyone in the German army or the SS agreed with what Hitler was doing," my father explained. "Some of the officers who are here tried to stop the war by assassinating Hitler, and these brave men were forced to run for their lives when they failed."

"Are some of them real Nazis?" I asked.

He said, "Yes they are, and the Mossad [Israel's equivalent to the CIA] has found a number of the most wanted Nazis in Argentina and Chile. But no matter who we meet, we need to be polite to everyone because you never know what they went through during the war." Dad said this part sternly.

My dad built a special rack for the top of our Jeep that held our tent, mattresses, and some suitcases. We were traveling from Chillán, where we were living, down to the southern tip of Chile, camping along the way. Susan and I slept on top of the Jeep in the tent, and Mom and Dad inside the Jeep. It was like a funny two-story apartment.

We had permission from one landowner to camp in his field and swim in the little bay at the bottom of a cliff. I leaned out the window of the parked Jeep, stretching to listen to Dad's conversation with the man. I was very curious to know if he was German, and if so, was he a bad guy or a good guy? I knew it wasn't polite to ask, but I really wanted to know.

Dad opened the gate to the field and then climbed back into the Jeep. He drove slowly through the gate, then stopped again to close it; then he picked out a spot near the path down to the bay. We all had to pitch in and set up the tent, and then we could go swimming. That tent went up in record time. We were covered in dust from driving on dirt roads all day, dust so thick on our faces that when we smiled, the dirt cracked and fell off in chunks. We all looked pretty funny, especially Mom, because she was just as dirty as we were, and she never got that dirty.

Down the cliff we climbed to find a charming inlet with a beach all the way around it. It was lovely, with soft waves and an awesome view of the ocean. I stuck a toe in the water and was happy to find it was warm. Once

I knew that, I waded out a ways and dove in.

Susan joined me and we had a ball swimming. It was so nice to get out of the hot Jeep and just have fun. We had been on the road since six o'clock in the morning to do at least part of our traveling in the cooler morning air, and it was now four in the afternoon—a very long day to sit bumping along unpaved, dusty roads. Our behinds were sore all over.

Susan called out over the roar of the water, "We've been invited to dinner at the owner's house, so Mom wants us to wash up!"

I started to swim for shore to get some soap when a shiny black head popped up right in front of me! I was nose to nose with two big black eyes, an impressive set of whiskers, and the worst fish breath I had ever smelled. What the heck was a seal doing this far north?

Suddenly, he shook the water out of his eyes and sneezed all over me. It was gross, but also very funny, and I started to laugh. I swear he smiled at me and then he imitated as best he could the sound of my laughter. I couldn't help but giggle some more. There we were, nose to nose, laughing like old buddies.

I felt no fear of him, and he was equally unafraid of me. He flipped over on his back, matching my floating position. Then he looked at me slyly and made that chuckling sound again. I swam toward shore and he swam along beside me, adding loops under and around me quick as lightning. He reached out his nose and bumped me gently.

Mindful that he was wild, I cautiously reached out toward him to let him sniff my hand the way I always did when I met a new dog. He inched his nose toward my hand; at first it was a gentle sniff, then he looked up at me, reached back to my hand, and gave an enormous snuffle. He put his flippers over his face and peered out at me from between them. I was laughing so hard I was afraid I might drown.

Suddenly my father was there beside me. Dad was a certified lifeguard and a fast swimmer. In a calm, quiet voice he said, "Remember, Nance, he is wild."

"I'm not so sure, Dad," I gasped. "He makes expressions and does stuff that makes me think he's been around humans before." Just as I said that the seal ducked his head under the sea, shoveled water with his head, and splashed us both.

Shaking the water out of his eyes, my dad couldn't help but laugh. He waved toward the shore to reassure Mother, who was standing there looking worried.

We swam with that seal for an hour. I had to go to the beach every now and then to rest, and he followed me ashore. Animals had always been drawn to me, and countless lost dogs had followed me home. My mom swore I was walking around with hot dogs in my pockets, I was so popular with canines, but I had never imagined that a seal would follow me. I sat on the sand and he sat down right beside me, looking at me expectantly, as if I was going to come up with a new game that would be fun to play. When nothing interesting happened, he stretched out beside me to sun himself.

Susan and Mother came over to sit near him. He waddled over to say hello and filled the air with his funny chuckling sound. He was clearly enjoying himself. Mother handed me some soap and told me to clean up. Back into the water I went followed by my flipper buddy. It was such an amazing experience that I didn't want it to stop ever, but we had to go to our host's house for dinner.

As I climbed up the cliff, my new friend followed me to the bottom of the path, and then he wailed as he watched me ascend the rest of the way. He made the saddest sound and I felt awful. Who wanted to go to a dumb dinner instead of playing with a seal? I had to be polite; after all, we were camping in the man's field, but I grumbled to myself all the way up the cliff.

At the house, the people seemed nice, but my mind was still on the seal. We ate in a big dining room with an enormous table. We were introduced to so many of our host's cousins and grandchildren, it made my head spin. After dinner we sat in their living room, next to another room with windows all around. An older woman, who seemed pretty frail, sat in that room making lace with her hands. Her face and arms were scarred, and earlier I had seen her walking with the support of a cane. She used a little gadget made of bone, and as her hands flew back and forth, a line of beautiful lace flowed into her lap. I was fascinated.

The adults in the living room were talking about boring stuff, and I wanted to know what she was doing, so I snuck closer. She looked up at me, her eyes twinkling, and she beckoned me over, patted a big stool next to her chair and then reached into her sewing box and pulled out a plastic version of the bone thing she was using. She wound the cord she was using on the plastic device and offered it to me. Slowly she showed me the moves she was using, and I tried to duplicate them.

When I messed up, she gently took my hands and showed me how to move them. I was producing a ragged version of her lace, and I was so excited. She said something in a language I didn't understand. I tried answering her in English, but she shook her head no. I tried Spanish, and she made a motion to signify she could speak it a little. One of this woman's relatives, a girl older than me, came in and sat down next to me, and she started translating.

"Rose wants you to know that you're very good for someone doing this the first time," the girl told me.

I looked down at my raggedy mess and shook my head no. Both of them laughed, and Rose said something that the girl translated. "She says her first attempt was a disaster. She's been doing this since she was your age, and she wants you to have the shuttle and cord, so you can practice and learn how to do it well."

"Thank you! That is so nice of you," I said as I held up my ragged-looking lace, "but I doubt I'll ever be any good at it." Then I said to Rose, "What language are you speaking?"

The younger girl said, "Rose speaks Austrian, German, French, Italian, Hungarian, and a little bit of Spanish. She came over here from Europe after the war, and she's had a hard time learning Spanish."

I said, "Wow! I can't imagine knowing that many languages! I only speak English and Spanish, and I'm learning French in school."

"You have plenty of time to learn more languages," Rose's young relative said, adding that her name was Ines.

I told them about my swimming adventures with the wild seal. The girl translated for Rose, and they both seemed surprised. "We've never seen a seal there before. Rose wants to know, do animals always love you?"

The question surprised me, but I said, "Yes, my dad says animals are naturally attracted to me."

The older woman dropped her hands to her lap and seemed downcast. I didn't know what I had said to upset her. "I'm sorry," I said to Ines. "I didn't mean to make Rose sad."

Rose said something and the girl listened closely before she translated for me.

"Oh, no, no, no, it's fine," Ines said to me. "Rose's sister, Lily, was like that with animals, and it makes her sad to talk about her sister. She would like to tell you about her sister, though, because you are so like her. Their mother named them for her favorite flowers, the rose and the lily. They were identical twins."

Rose reached into her apron pocket and drew out a framed photograph, which she offered to me. In the photo, sitting side-by-side on a rock wall, were two beautiful little twin girls.

"They look exactly the same," I said. "How could anyone tell them apart?"

Rose laughed and spoke at length. Ines translated, "Rose says, 'We used to have a lot of fun tricking everybody when we changed places. We lived in a villa in Austria. Father was a banker, and his brother was a jeweler. Mother was a concert pianist, and our house was always full of music and interesting guests.'"

Rose stopped for a bit to dab at tears that had begun trickling down her face. Such a sad face. I did not dare say a thing.

Ines continued with the translation. "Those were our happiest days, and then the Germans came. Father packed us up and we fled, taking what little we could carry. We tried to stay ahead of the Nazis, and we succeeded in hiding for quite a while. One day they caught up to us, loaded us into cattle cars, and took us to this terrible camp." Ines talked to Rose briefly.

Rose shook her head.

Ines said, "I asked her if she really wanted to talk about this with you, because she doesn't talk about it with strangers. Then she said the strangest thing; she said she wanted to tell you her story because you are like Lily, and she believes that you will one day tell many people about her story. She wants the world to never forget the awful things that happened. I also told her I was worried that you were too young to hear this story, but she insisted that you have a lot of courage and you can handle this just fine."

I felt my father sit down beside me. He said, "What this lady has gone through is very difficult, but I think we should honor her by listening, even though I think it will upset you to hear her story."

I looked at Dad in surprise and asked, "How do you know what her story is? I thought you had never met these people before."

"I haven't met them before, Nance, but I have read stories about what happened to people in concentration camps. It's up to you if you want to hear about it because the things that happened were horrible, and I don't want you to be damaged by that."

I looked at Rose as she sat waiting quietly to see what I would say. I looked in her eyes and said, "I would like to hear about Lily, if you don't mind telling me about it."

Ines translated what I had said, and Rose smiled and reached out to pat my hands. Very slowly she said, "Sank you." Taking a deep breath, Rose began her story, pausing occasionally so Ines could translate.

"We were unloaded in the dead of night. It was so dark, we couldn't see where we were. I remember the soldiers with the big dogs who patrolled the walkways. The dogs snapped and snarled at us as if they wanted to eat us. Lily and I were terrified, and father and grandfather stood between us and the dogs so we would feel safer. The soldiers laughed at our fear, and that made it even scarier.

"Father and Grandfather were dragged away from us, and Lily and I clung to our mother as she held us close. We were crying and so was Mother. It was all too terrifying, and we were just young girls who had led a privileged and protected life until then.

"A man with medals on his chest and shiny, tall boots barked orders at the soldiers as he walked down the line of people. He said his words so quickly that we couldn't understand him; we were just learning German. Mother understood what he was saying and told us quietly that surely soon he would realize the mistake, and he would let us go home. Inside, I knew she was wrong, and I think Lily did too. Lily and I had always been able to sense what was coming, not just for ourselves but overall."

Ines stopped translating and said directly to me, "That's why Rose says you're like Lily. Because she was the same way with animals that you are, and she also knew things that she shouldn't have known anything about, like you do."

I was startled. "How did Rose know that?"

"Rose has always just known things," Ines answered. "My father says because of all the suffering she's had, her brain found a way to figure out what to do to survive, and the skill is still there."

Rose resumed her story, and Ines continued to relay it to me. "When the officer came near us, he stopped and stared at Lily and me. He motioned toward Mother and pointed in one direction, and then he turned his finger toward us and waved in a different direction. Mother started to wail as if her heart was breaking. The soldiers grabbed her and dragged her away."

We waited because Rose was overcome with grief.

"We never saw our mother, father, or grandfather again. We heard later that Mother and Grandfather were gassed the first day and that our father survived doing forced labor for quite a while before he died of malnutrition. Lily and I were taken to a hospital and put in the hands of a doctor who told us he was conducting research on how to heal battlefield wounds more quickly, and he needed identical twins for his study. We were locked in a large ward with a lot of other identical twins. As Lily and I walked to the beds assigned to us, we noticed that in each set of twins there was one healthy twin and one twin who was dying. Lily and I held onto each other, terrified about what was going to happen to us.

"Early the next morning the doctor greeted us, and then he took both of us away to an operating room. He put us to sleep, and when we woke up we each had terrible wounds on one leg. It hurt so bad that we both cried, and the nurses came and gave us medicine that put us to sleep. Every now and then I would wake up and see that Lily was getting sicker and sicker, but somehow I was okay. The wounds hurt terribly, but mine were healing and hers were not. We realized that the difference in our treatment was that they were putting some kind of powder on my wounds and not on Lily's. At night after the ward was locked up we took off our bandages, and I took some of the powder off of my leg and put it on hers. We did our best to put the bandages back the way they were, but we got caught.

"They put us both in restraints, so I couldn't help Lily anymore. They punished me by leaving me there to watch her die. At night I sang to her the songs our mother had played for us on the piano. We wondered where Mother was, and if she was all right. Most of the time we were in dreadful pain and terrified.

"The last night Lily and I were humming to each other softly and holding hands stretched across the space between our beds. She stopped humming, her breathing got ragged, and then it stopped completely. I kept holding her hand as long as I could, crying quietly because I was now completely alone. I thought they would hold a funeral for her, and I would get to go. Instead, they dumped her body in a wheelbarrow, and the last I saw of her was her hand hanging over the side.

"I was cared for on that ward until my leg wounds healed. They left me horribly scarred." Rose reached down and pulled her long skirt up to show me the mutilation. It was ghastly. It looked like someone had dug a trench in her leg along her calf bone. "As you can see, the doctor's work is not pretty. The last day I was in the ward, he pinned a small medal to my pajama top and thanked me for my service to the Reich. I had no idea what he was talking about.

"From there I was sent to a camp building where I was made available to the soldiers for their sexual pleasure. I was grateful that Lily had not lived to see it. One of the soldiers took a liking to me, and it was he who told me what happened to my mother and the rest of my family. At that point I was so weak and malnourished that although I cried for hours, there were no tears.

"There are those who are trying to say that these things did not happen, but they did, and I believe it's important for the world to remember that they did." She reached out and held my hands tight because I was crying for her and Lily.

With a smile, Rose said her parting words to me: "Do not worry. That enemy was defeated and I survived and so many of my family survived. I have had a good life since then."

My parents, sister, and I returned to the pasture where we had set up camp. I climbed up into the top-level tent with Susan, and exhausted from swimming with the seal and from the emotion of hearing Rose's story, I fell asleep right away. I woke suddenly to feel the ground shaking under me. I screamed, "Earthquake!" and headed for the opening of the tent.

Dad called out to me, "It's not an earthquake. Look out the tent flap and you'll see what it is."

The tent continued to shake and I could hear Mother and Dad laughing. I also heard what sounded like a panicked cow mooing over and over. The ties on the tent flap were damp and stubborn; Susan and I couldn't untie them easily. Once we got them open we saw in the early morning light that Dad was standing by the driver's side window trying to help a cow get her head unstuck from the aperture. Obviously, someone forgot we were there and let the whole herd loose in the pasture around our car. The cows surrounded our Jeep, licking the dew off the sides and windows and causing an "earthquake."

Dad freed Mrs. Cow from the window, and she ran away terrified. The landowner came out on horseback and apologized for the mistake. His wife had made sandwiches for our trip that day, and he also had a bottle of milk that Rose had given him to give to me. We put the milk and sandwiches in the cooler and climbed down the cliff for one last swim before another hot day of driving.

I never told my parents that when Rose related the story of her life in the concentration camp, I saw the whole thing unfold in my mind, like a movie. For years afterward I saw the reruns of those horrors in my dreams—the experiments Rose underwent, the torture in the brothel from the soldiers that permanently damaged her inside so that she could never have children, nor could she stand to be touched by men, other than the helping hands of family members. How could anyone be so monstrous as to treat children that way?

It wasn't the first time I had had visions, but my previous visualizations had been about my own future. This was the first time I had seen someone else's past. I was too young to understand what was happening, and as children often do, I took it in stride and figured that one day maybe I would better understand what I had seen.

Chapter 9
My Growing Abilities

When we returned to Chillán, I realized that something had happened to me when I listened to Rose's story. For some time I dreamed of her ordeal every night. It was a nightmare but not the kind that makes a person wake up screaming in fear. The nightmare was the realization that human beings can be unmitigated monsters. Until Rose told me of her childhood, I didn't know that people, especially those so young, could be tortured in such a horrible way. I struggled to try to understand war, murder, and brutality, but it made no sense to me.

My search for understanding led me to read about the Nazis and what they had done. Mother became concerned because I seemed obsessed with it. She tried to talk to me about it, but I could not tell her what I felt. It was my dad who finally got me to talk.

Dad's favorite place to go for a serious talk, no matter where we lived, was out in the countryside. We drove out to a dirt road next to a horse paddock. He parked in the shade of a row of eucalyptus trees and pulled out a picnic lunch Mom had packed for us. Dad got out a thermos and poured his favorite Southern sweet iced tea into big plastic cups. It was magical for me to sit with the breeze blowing softly through the eucalyptus trees, making them clatter and causing the lovely smell to surround us. I loved having my dad all to myself. I knew we were there to have a talk, but time with him was wonderful, even if I was in trouble for something. I brushed the thought aside, munched my sandwich, and sipped cold iced tea.

Dad's lunch disappeared quickly. Mother was always fussing for him to stop eating so fast. He wiped his hands on his clean red bandana and turned to stare at me. Here it comes! I ducked my head and focused on my sandwich as my mind raced through my latest scrapes trying to figure out which one had provoked the talking-to I was about to get. I couldn't think of what it was, as I had been busy reading and I couldn't remember doing anything wrong.

"Your mother is worried about you and all this interest in the Nazis," he began. "We think that we shouldn't have let you hear Rose's story because you're too young to handle it. But you did hear it, so maybe I can do something to help you understand it better."

I looked up in surprise. I was in the clear! I hadn't done anything wrong! In fact, I was relieved to talk with Dad about this subject because it was upsetting, and I needed to ask some important questions. My heart lifted and I was able to swallow the lump of sandwich that had stuck in my throat the minute he started talking in such a serious tone.

I asked him what had been on my mind: "Why didn't anyone stop it?"

Dad sat there thoughtfully for a moment. "For a long time, no one outside Germany knew what was happening. Once Hitler attacked other countries and expanded his empire, he started building the concentration camps. Word leaked out about them when refugees fled Nazi terror. At first it was hard to believe anyone could commit atrocities like that. A lot of what happened was hidden until the concentration camps were liberated, although there had been some aerial reconnaissance that showed trains full of people that were not troops—women and even babies were seen in the trains. Later, the survivors of these camps told their stories to the world, and the extent of how monstrous it had been became known. I've read about things like what Rose went through, but I had never met anyone who survived it."

As he spoke there was such sadness in my father's face. I had never seen him look like that before. I thought maybe I shouldn't ask any more questions because it made him so sad.

Dad continued, "Rose's cousin, the man who owned that house we visited, told me that she rarely spoke of it, and even he had never heard the full account of what happened to Lily until the night that she told you about it. Her relatives were in shock that she told her story to a complete stranger. But I think I know why she did it. Somehow, she knew about your abilities, and I think she believed that you would have the courage to speak for her.

He paused. "But your mother's right that this could be too much for you. You're only eight going on nine. We think it would be a good idea if you stop reading about what the Nazis did for a while and get some distance from it." He paused again. "What do you think?"

I had to collect my thoughts for a minute before I answered him. "As Rose was telling me her story, I could see it in my head. I know it was real because it came to me like my visions always do, in the same way I can see what I will be doing when I grow up.

"Remember I told you about that time I was sitting on a bench near the bocce court in Brazil and that lady came over and showed me what my job was going to look like when I grew up? I was standing in front of a lot of people and I was talking to them about my life and they liked that.

"That's the first time I remember such a thing. It's happened a bunch of times since then, but the visions of Rose's life were so terrible, I can't get them out of my head. I keep reading about the Nazis and the war, hoping that I can understand it better, but now I think there is no way to understand it. Some people are just evil, and somehow I know that when I grow up I want to help catch bad people and put them where they can't hurt anybody. I've seen visions where I do things like that, but I can't figure out *how* I'm doing it. Dad, do you know how I could do it?" I asked.

Dad said, "No, I have no idea how you will do it. But I know you will. Any time you need to talk about this you come and tell me, okay?"

I said I would.

"Is there anything else you need to talk about?" he asked. My dad always knew when something was bothering me.

In Chillán there were several tribes of Gypsies that always hung around the market area, trying to sell goats and telling fortunes. They dressed differently from the local people and had really piercing eyes. I felt like they were looking right through me. They kept talking in their language around me and pointing at me and following me. It was getting steadily worse.

"The Gypsies are following me again," I told him, "and that scares me. Our maids tell me that when they're interested in children, they steal them sometimes. Is that true?"

They had followed me home from the market one day when I was with Maria, our maid, and now I couldn't go out to walk my Beagle Samba alone because there were always two or three Gypsy children watching the house. The minute I would come out, they'd run around the corner and then return with a bunch of ladies who touched my hair and my face as they babbled away. It was so scary for me.

Everything I had heard about Gypsies described them as people known to cause trouble around Chillán.

He nodded. "I have heard Maria talk about that, and I know she is frightened too. I already told Maria to call the Carabineros if anything like it happens again. I'll talk to Captain Delgado, my friend on the force, and see what he thinks we should do. I'm quite sure the Gypsies won't harm you. You and Susan are the only American girls in all of southern Chile right now, and I think they're just curious, but you both must always be with an adult when you go out, just to be safe." He reached out and rumpled my hair.

"Dad, I'm getting too big for that!" I protested.

We loaded the remains of our picnic in the Jeep and drove back home in silence. I could feel that Dad was more worried about the Gypsies than he let on. I also knew that he would take care of it. I fixed my hair and watched the dust from the dirt road billow into the air and surround our car. We had closed the windows even though it was hot, because we had not had rain in at least a week and the dust was terrible.

When we got home, we unloaded the picnic gear and left it on the counter in the kitchen. Dad gave me a big hug and went outside to work on the tile roof. The cats had knocked the tiles loose again, and the roof was leaking. The fact that he was going to talk to his police friend was reassuring. I knew he would make sure I was safe.

The next morning was market day, and I wanted to go with Maria to do the shopping. The market was a wonderful place full of animals of all kinds—sometimes even small cougars! The Indians came down from the mountains with their beautiful ponchos and sombreros and laid out their wares on the ground to attract buyers. The market overflowed with silver jewelry, clothing, fruits, and vegetables. Customers could buy cows, pigs, burros, or goats for their farms. The pigs were the most fun because they were escape artists and always running through the marketplace, right through all the goods displayed on the ground. People ran after them with willow switches, trying to keep pigs out of everyone's merchandise. Farmers, kids, goods, and pigs went flying everywhere, and the spectators would laugh, whistle, and pretend to root for the pigs.

Some buyers had their animals butchered right there and loaded into their trucks. Watching the butchering was scary, but having been around farming all my life, I had learned to tolerate it. The smell of fresh oranges, fresh meat, and animal dung added to the ambiance of the day.

The very best thing was watching ranchers sell gorgeous horses. Most were just regular cart horses, but some days there were beautiful, shiny, and sleek race horses and huge, strong, acrobatic horses the size of Percherons. Sometimes there were even polo ponies. Their owners would take them into a corral off to the side and put them through their paces. I loved to watch the acrobatic horses leap into the air, all four hooves off the ground. When they landed the earth shook, and with their nostrils flaring and necks arching it was a magical spectacle. The Chileans were famous for their horsemanship, and they bred incredible animals that people from all over the world came to buy, some days Germans, other days Arabs in long, flowing robes. The market was much too interesting for me to miss because of a bunch of scary Gypsies. Besides, I knew Daddy's Carabinero friend would make them go away, or he would arrest them. No, I was not missing the market.

As we approached the marketplace I stayed close to Maria, which normally I would have done anyway. But already the Gypsy children were following us. All of a sudden, an old Gypsy man I had seen before approached us, dressed fancier than the rest of his people—in black velvet pants and a vest. Silver buttons trimmed his vest and the side of his pants. His hat looked like the kind Flamenco dancers wore, but he tied an odd bandana around his head under the hat. His eyes looked black, his curly hair peeked out all around the bandana, and he had a narrow mustache. He wore rings on the fingers of both hands, and he shooed people out of his way with a dismissive wave. The man bowed formally to me and spoke in the Romani language, smiling with his mouth but not his eyes. His grown son, a taller, thinner, handsomer version of his father, smiled gently at me and translated, "My father asks if you know that you are a star child?"

Maria put her arm around me and scolded the men for approaching me, despite the fact that I could feel her shaking with fear.

The son said, "My father means you no harm, and he has told the children to stop following you." To demonstrate his authority the older man waved at the Gypsy children, and they scattered.

"My father is the king of the Gypsies and he heard about you from the children. He says you have stars all around your head, and he wants you to know that one day you will be a great seer. Did you know that?" the man asked.

Maria was growing ever more nervous. In whichever direction the Gypsy king and his son moved, she kept pace with them and made sure she stood between them and me.

I said, "I have no idea what you're talking about. My father doesn't want you around me." I hoped my fear did not come across in my voice. Despite all his pretensions, this man knew that he should not be bothering me—and I knew it too. In the Chilean culture Gypsies would never approach the children of what would be considered upper-class families. And I was an American girl, so he knew he was crossing a social line. I could feel the adults around me in the market reacting to his boldness. They showed their displeasure by emitting low hisses at the Gypsies, which had the effect of emboldening me. My instinct was to do my best to show no fear. I squared my shoulders and tried to stare him down. He clearly never expected someone as young as me to show that kind of bravery.

The older man spoke a bit, and his son listened and then translated: "My father says he is extending his protection to you, and the children and women will stop following you. But it is important that you understand what you are. Have you had any visions yet?"

I wondered how he knew. "I've had some," I allowed. Before Christmas or birthdays I often dreamt about what I would get—which to a child kind of spoiled the gift. If I was going to get to see a really neat animal, I would dream about it a week or so in advance. There was even a time that I dreamt about the death of someone I knew months before it happened. And of course I had just talked to Dad about the visions near the bocce court in Brazil. I realized I had already had quite a few episodes.

The king spoke again and his son translated: "You will have many more visions, and you will have many talents, including healing."

At that moment, I was relieved to see Captain Delgado hurrying across the market toward us, a scowl on his face, his hand on his holster, and his sword clanging against his leg. I knew he would make sure I was safe.

"What's going on here?" the officer barked. Captain Delgado was tall for a Chilean, and he pulled up to his full height as he glared at the gypsies. He had strawberry blonde hair and looked like an Englishman. His coloring was most unusual for a Chilean, but it was said his people descended from a section of Spain where blonde coloring was common. He looked especially handsome in his uniform, and I figured there must be some important people coming to the market today. I always enjoyed watching him because I had a crush on him.

"Nothing is going on, your honor," said the son. "My father just wanted to meet this talented young lady and offer her his protection. He means no harm, and when he offers his protection, no Gypsies will bother her."

"That's a good thing because she is under *my* protection," said Delgado. "I had better not hear of anymore harassment from Gypsies."

The Gypsy king doffed his hat and bowed to me, and then the two men departed.

I wondered how he knew about my visions. My father was the only person I had told about them, and I knew he didn't discuss them with anybody but my mother. I had begun to see things that would happen in my future. I had dreams about being an author, which made me happy because I was already writing stories. I also had a vision that I would get typhoid fever, and my illness would make me miss a dance recital I had practiced so hard for. What bothered me most about this vision was that the little girl who replaced me got to wear my costume. I did not want to share that pretty little outfit my mother had made for me, but when the time came, that is exactly what happened.

Maria always said that Gypsies know things that no one tells them, and I decided it must be true. I wished it were safe for me to talk to the Gypsy king again; maybe he could tell me more about what he meant about the stars around me and my visions. Maybe he could help me answer my own questions. But I would just have to wait for the day when I could understand all this better.

Chapter 10
The Garden of Gethsemane

The day had not gone as expected. I had begun to get a little notoriety for my work as an investigator. At my home in Newark, I had received two calls from individuals who claimed to be Christians threatening me because I was psychic. It wasn't the first time this happened, and I was sure it would not be the last. Experience had taught me that reasoning with prejudiced people like this never worked.

The teachings these people followed did not allow for my existence, and their beliefs encouraged them to discriminate against people who were different from them. It amazed me that in trying to convert me to their views, they lost sight of Jesus's teachings in the New Testament about not judging people unfairly. They could not see the contradiction between their assertion that they were Christians and their objectionable behavior.

I had read a small book written by the Dalai Lama, which contained a variety of spiritual teachings, such as the Golden Rule, and described how different religions presented these concepts. The book left me aware that basic teachings, although phrased differently, were the same across religions. I took that to mean these lessons came from the same spiritual source and were adjusted to fit different cultures.

In my childhood lived around the world, I had been exposed to multiple religions and had heard many stories of miracles. I had doubted these stories when I was younger, yet now they made perfect sense considering my growing understanding of the Light of Life and the unity it creates for anyone who wishes to acknowledge it.

The powerful transformational experience I had in Gethsemane often recurred in my mind, and each time I relived it I understood it a little better. How blind I had been for most of my life. With my father as my guide to understanding the Light of Life, I was experiencing another transformation, this one more gradual than what I had felt at Gethsemane but just as life changing.

I tried to reach out to those attacking me by talking about the gifts of God and how the Bible instructs us to judge people by their work, which in my career meant helping to put murderers behind bars. Every now and then I found someone who was able to understand the incongruity of judging others, but this day that did not happen.

It was the anniversary of my Father's death, Halloween, and I had just completed work on another case involving the murder of a child. My sensitive nature made it especially hard to work on murder cases and continue to have faith in humanity as the unimaginable horrors perpetrated by a few criminals assaulted me. Only my deep faith in God enabled me to do the work I did, and then I had to put up with people telling me I was the instrument of the devil. I did not feel strong enough to deal with this.

Although the murder investigation had gone well, the case was an emotional nightmare. My eyes swam with tears brought on by strain and exhaustion and by the horrendous images of the death of the little six-year-old girl in the case I'd just finished. Through my weariness I felt my dad's hand on my shoulder and heard him say, "Don't forget Gethsemane and what you felt that day." The moment I heard his words my mind replayed that day in the blinding sunlight when I found myself rooted to a particular spot in the Garden, and I was ashamed of my surrender to weakness.

It was Easter vacation, too short a time to go back home for most of us in the boarding department at the American Community School in Beirut, Lebanon, so the school arranged a number of trips for us to choose from. A trip to Moscow to see the Bolshoi was most appealing because of my love of ballet, but thinking about going behind the Iron Curtain terrified me. Visiting the pyramids in Egypt was another choice, but for a reason that was unclear to me, I decided on the trip to the Holy Land. I had many questions about that part of ancient history, and I knew with my heightened abilities, I could pick up details from archaeological sites, as I had done in Afghanistan. That is how I came to be in Jordan with three busloads of cynical American teenagers who had travelled extensively and were anything but interested in the touristy sites we had already visited prior to reaching the Church of All Nations. Here, the teenage babble quieted down. Even the most scoffing among us seemed to sense something profound about this simple beautiful church with the spectacular mosaic of Jesus praying at the rock on the night of his arrest. We entered the church in silence and stood staring at the huge, amazing artwork.

After some time inside, I came out of the darkened Church of All Nations and walked directly into blinding sunlight and what a guide had told me was the historic location of the Garden of Gethsemane. Its withered, ancient olive trees mingled eerily with carefully tended white stone pathways. The sun beat down fiercely on those stones, its reflection nearly painful to my eyes.

When I walked into the convergence of four wide paths, silence fell abruptly and I was unable to move. I stood rooted to the stones; suddenly it was night and I was all alone. The burning sun disappeared and darkness pressed in on me. I felt weight—the weight of the world—on my shoulders. Not far away, voices broke the silence and shadowy figures moved around a small fire. I could not see the people clearly, but the voices were male. Tears coursed down my face, the result of being overtaken with grief. A sickening kiss on my cheek doubled me over as pain crashed through me. I cried out and reached toward the fleeing figure that had kissed me, but I was surrounded by menacing-looking men wearing metal breastplates and pointing spears at me.

The blinding sunlight returned as suddenly as it had disappeared. A hideous weight caused pain to sear through my body as I struggled to breathe. I felt gentle hands prevent me from falling over. My eyes gradually adjusted to the bright sun, and I found myself surrounded by a number of priests wearing black cassocks and holding notebooks. I was stricken with panic but I remained fixed to the spot with pain still coursing through me. Gasping for breath and struggling to stand up straight under the mighty weight, I felt those gentle hands steady me once again. It was as if pure love flowed from these unknown hands and into my heart. I looked down where I felt the hands and realized that nothing was holding me, yet I felt a strong grip bracing me so I would not fall over. A calm voice spoke to me in a language I had never heard before, yet I understood it. It was a male voice, so kind, and its softness calmed the horrible pain. The voice said, "Give the pain back to me. This pain is not yours to bear. I will always be with you, and you will work with me as one who knows."

I felt those gentle hands lift the burden and the pain that had doubled me over. I had no idea how any human being could survive that weight for long. In the distance I heard insistent voices asking me questions in different languages. I longed to remain in the embrace of the gentle hands that comforted me, but the babble of these robed men drew me back into the daylight. I recognized those hands instinctively and did not want to be without them.

The priests' questions prevailed. They tried speaking in different languages, desperate to know if I was all right and what I had experienced. I turned toward a priest who spoke English with an American Southern accent and begged, "Please stop scaring me!" He spoke to the rest of the priests who had been pressing in on me. They backed away and quieted. The Southerner took over the questions.

"Can you share with us what you just experienced?" he asked gently.

At just 16 years of age, I had not been sure that God was real. I had struggled with my feelings about that for a long time. Now, I was at peace with the knowledge that He *was* real. I knew with no reservations that Jesus suffered terrible pain at the betrayal of Judas. I felt a modicum of that pain when I somehow crossed into another time and ran into that appalling experience. How this could have happened I had no way to understand, but I was quite certain that my mind had traveled back in time to experience that fateful night in Jesus's life, and that I had felt the kiss of betrayal and the anguish it caused. The force of this knowledge was greater than anything I had ever experienced. I was forever transformed from someone who doubted to someone who knew with certainty that Jesus lived and God was real.

I had gone back to a previous age in an instant. It was as though events were somehow recorded in the ethos, and my psychic mind enabled me to revisit the past just by being in the right spot on the earth. I had actually done it before and seen slices of history as if I were watching a movie as a spectator. But this time I was blindsided by what I had witnessed and what I had felt. It meant that this was the exact spot where the betrayal occurred so long ago. All I could manage to gasp was, "He is real! I felt His gentle hands and His horrible pain! This must really be the Garden of Gethsemane!"

Questions flew from all of the priests at once. They all spoke English apparently, and their bombardment overwhelmed me. "Stop, please stop!" I pleaded. "Let me absorb what just happened."

The Southern priest said, "This has happened to others in the Garden. We try to document any such experiences so that we can learn about this. Can you tell us what you felt?"

The words emerged slowly. "I felt the most excruciating sadness I've ever experienced, then a man kissed me on the cheek and the pain overwhelmed me." In recounting it, I found myself rubbing my cheek where the horrible kiss had landed. "A crushing weight forced me toward the ground. I started to fall when I felt gentle hands holding onto me and I heard a soothing voice tell me to give Him back the pain as it was not mine to bear. That gentle soul. How could Judas betray Him like that?" Someone handed me a handkerchief and a glass of water. I gulped that water as if I had been in the desert for days.

What the priest had said earlier found its way into my brain and I asked him, "Others have experienced this?"

"Every once in a while someone feels what you have felt," he said. "It is always in this spot. That is why there are always priests here to help the person and to record what is happening. Do you understand what happened to you?"

With no hesitation I said, "I felt the kiss of betrayal! It was so horrible it surpassed any nightmare I've ever had. Then Jesus lifted that pain off me and helped me to stand again." A crowd had gathered around us. Everyone was listening to the priests' questions and my answers. I grew embarrassed and knew I had to get back to the bus so I did not get left behind. I tried to push through the priests, but they stood firm.

"Please don't go," said the priest with a hand on my arm. "Help us to understand what happened to you."

"How am I supposed to explain what happened? I don't understand it myself! One minute I was here, the next minute I was in another time experiencing the betrayal of Jesus. Now, you tell me: How that can happen? You are the religious experts!"

The priests remained silent. They had no answers, or they weren't sharing what they did know. They all blessed me as I walked away to rejoin my group. I noticed that some of my teachers and fellow students had been listening to my discussion with the priests. I didn't care what they might think about me. I hugged the experience to me and found strength in it.

The emotional memory of that day faded as my mind returned to the present. I had hidden away that experience in my heart and soul, but I knew it had made my abilities stronger than they had ever been before. I never talked about it, except with my father, the one person who understood my gift, and the person who had reminded me of what I had experienced many years before.

I had been struggling with my emotions over the murder of a beautiful child and the evil the killer displayed to his helpless victim. Then I had received cruel threats from people who could not and would not ever understand how dedicated to God I had to be in order to even do this work. But Dad had helped me to remember the gentle comfort of those hands in the Garden and the soft whispered words, "Give back the pain. It is not yours to bear." As I had on that day when I was 16, I felt the pain leave and

I became strong enough to withstand it all.

How can I explain to non-psychic people my father's ghost holding the most normal, everyday conversation with me in my living room? How do I describe that long-ago vision at Gethsemane without the world thinking I am weird? Perhaps God wanted me to feel the suffering Jesus felt so that I would always remember that no matter what suffering I had to go through, it was a tiny amount of what Jesus endured. These events did occur; they are real. Dad still exists in some form, and as part of the Light of Life, he drops in for visits. I just have to remember his comforting words when the going is rough. And I must stay strong so that I can continue to lead people to find greater purpose and happiness in their lives, and to help law enforcement to solve criminal cases.

In the Garden that day I was shown what I would become, but I had no way of understanding the meaning of the images that sped before my eyes. I saw murdered people and murderers being put away where they could no longer hurt others. I saw myself speaking to auditoriums full of people who sought to know more about life through what I could share. Although I understood that those scenes flashing through my head related to work I would do someday, for the moment it was unfathomable to me. Inside myself I agreed to take on the difficult job of learning how to use my gifts and dedicate myself to helping people, not harming them. I believe that my courage and willingness to take on this job without a full understanding of what it would mean for me is the reason that God gave me these gifts. Why He chose me still puzzles me because I did not think I was a remarkable person. I had difficulties in perception that made learning to read and do math a struggle. I was simply a well-traveled American teenager trying to figure out what she wanted to be when she grew up. I'm not always strong and I'm stubborn. In my mind I often find myself trying to convince God that I'm not as tough as He thinks I am. Each time I have been tested, however, I have managed to rise to the occasion.

Chapter 11

The Missing Child

It was nasty-cold outside. I was sick of being pregnant, yet after the miscarriages, I was so glad that this time it was sticking. But it would be nice if she would come out, since I was nearly a month past my due date. There was no such thing as a comfortable position for sitting or sleeping. Her busy feet beat a steady rhythm on a particular left rib, making that rib so sore that every time she started kicking, I would try to push her feet away from the spot. There would be a long pause, then swish, swish and she'd be back at my rib. I got up because I found that walking around eased the pain from her endless thumping. I was so ready for her to arrive.

The phone rang. It was Detective Greg Sacco from the unit of the Delaware State Police nicknamed the Sherlock Squad. I had worked a lot of cases with Greg and his partner. After some polite questions about the tardy baby and how I was feeling, he told me an autistic child had disappeared the day before from a care center downstate, and he wondered if I felt up to helping locate the child. More than merely saying yes, I offered to go down there by helicopter to help.

After Greg got through laughing at me he said, "Nancy, do you honestly think any of us want to take that chance with you and end up delivering a baby?"

"I was hoping," I responded, rubbing my sore rib.

Greg told me that some of the child's possessions were being flown up by chopper for me to read, and he would bring these articles to my house as soon as possible. Any information I could glean from the items would be relayed to the teams that had already begun the search.

Within a half hour Greg, his partner, and a trooper who had brought the articles up in the helicopter sat in my living room; all three were in touch with search parties in the field by radio. The men handed me a large photo of a beautiful child with big, gorgeous eyes. He looked like he was about eight. They also had a sweater and the boy's favorite teddy bear. As I held these things, images started to run through my mind.

I knew at once that the child was dead. I had to fight a sudden urge to throw up. My father's voice spoke softly yet firmly in my head. "Steady, Nancy, you can do this. Help them find him."

Shivers ran through my body as I experienced the cold that the boy felt before he died. In my mind I saw him climbing way out on a tree limb and then falling into mud. Why couldn't the search party see him? Some of them were walking around his body.

"Three searchers are right next to him this second," I told the police officers. "I don't understand why they can't see him."

Greg asked me to describe the searchers. I visualized a man and a woman and described them and the jackets and hats they were wearing. The trooper radioed the details I had given to the search teams.

Suddenly I realized why they couldn't see the child. He had fallen into the mud up to his hips. He could not free himself and had lost consciousness due to the cold, causing him to fall forward. Fallen leaves had collected over his upper body until they covered him entirely, and all that was visible was the back of his head.

The trooper repeated into his radio what I was saying.

I advised, "Tell them to turn around and look low to the ground for his light-colored hair."

As that information was relayed, I heard a crackle from the radio and the voice of the trooper at the search site.

"We found him!" he shouted. "Tell Nancy thank you!"

The images of the boy ceased and the energy drained right out of me.

Tears flowed as I struggled for composure. As always, this kind of thing was hard to handle. I had so hoped in the beginning that I could help them find this innocent child alive, and the officers didn't know what to say to me. They were used to bad outcomes; I never got accustomed to it.

Once again my father's quiet voice filtered into my brain: "You helped to find him, Nance. They probably would never have seen him without your help. Be happy that at least you gave his parents an answer."

It was peculiar to hear my father's voice in my head, comforting me, while three policemen sat there worried about all the upset they had caused a nearly 10-months-pregnant woman.

I took a deep breath and grabbed a tissue. "Sorry about that, guys," I sniffed. "Being pregnant makes me awfully emotional. I wish you would have flown me down so this stubborn baby would arrive!"

On a sad day this produced a bit of laughter from all three men as they got up to leave, men who faced death regularly and understood that changing the subject and laughing were survival skills. It was something I was just learning.

As soon as they left, I threw up. It was the shock of seeing that lovely child dead in such a terrible, lonely way. I will forever remember that sweet boy's beautiful face. As I splashed cold water on my own face, I focused on anything available to try to escape the series of images that I had seen in my mind. I wished the trauma of it would set off labor. At least that would be a distraction, but my daughter-to-be was just not as ready as I was.

Chapter 12
Heidi

Not long after I helped find the body of the missing autistic boy I went into labor. At first I refused to go to the hospital. After all, I had already made several trips into Wilmington, only to have the labor stop once I arrived. I had this notion that *not* going to the hospital would change my luck. In a stern phone conversation, my doctor said that if I would not come voluntarily, he would send an ambulance.

Grudgingly, I got in the car and grumbled all the way there that I was sure we would be back home again soon. Christmas had just passed; at least she wouldn't have to share her birthday with the holiday. Upon arrival at the hospital, the doctor examined me and said with a smile tempered by self-satisfaction, "Nancy, you are in the final stage of labor. You are going to have a baby very shortly."

Heidi had other ideas, and "very shortly" turned into 24 hours. When she finally emerged, she was silent, and I feared the worst. The nurses and the pediatrician grabbed her and went to work to get her breathing.

Finally, she started bellowing and everyone cheered. I kept repeating, "It's a baby, it's a baby." My doctor laughed at me and asked me, "What did you think you had in there—a watermelon?" All of a sudden another contraction hit, and I had to start the Lamaze breathing all over again. The doctor said, "Nancy, you don't have to do the breathing anymore. You delivered her."

I ignored him and kept up the rhythmic breathing. The contraction was not as severe as it was in the previous stage before Heidi's birth, but it was strong enough. The doctor touched his hand to my belly, and a look of shock crossed his face. "I think we may have a second one," he said in surprise. The nurses positioned themselves to help as the contractions continued.

I was so exhausted I couldn't get excited about a second baby. I swooned during the hard end of the contractions, and the nurses worked to keep me focused. Finally, I felt my body release something, and I beheld a collection of bewildered faces. But I did not hear any crying. "Is the baby dead?" I gasped.

"It's not a baby," said the doctor, "it's a placenta." He dropped it in a basin and weighed it, whistled, and shook his head. "An eight-pound placenta," he said. "Never seen one quite like it. Usually they're only a couple of pounds." He turned to his nurse and quietly said, "Send that to pathology."

Finally, the nurses brought Heidi over and placed her on my chest. She was beautiful. Her little face was round; she had large, dark eyes and a tiny soft fluff of fuzzy hair just on the top of her head. I started to giggle because she looked like a Kewpie doll, and she studied me so seriously. I had chosen the name Heidi long before her birth, and now it seemed so appropriate. We stayed in the recovery room, Heidi and I together, staring at each other. It was now two hours after her birth, and she was still wide awake studying me. I felt such great peace holding her in my arms, but also a niggling fear that she would not survive. Still.

When the doctor came in, I said, "Something's wrong with her."

The pediatrician was right behind him, and the two of them took Heidi to a table and examined her from end to end.

"She's fine, Nancy," the pediatrician assured. "She's a beautiful, healthy baby girl. You've just been through too many disappointments, and that's making you nervous." I expected his reassurance that she was fine, but my intuition told me that something was wrong. So, I sat guard watching her, and she was still watching me.

Heidi was born at noon on December 28, 1976. Exactly 24 hours later as I fed her and talked to her, and as she studied me with those serious eyes, I saw her seize. The right side of her body jerked, yet she lay there calm and relaxed as if this were normal. It was clear that she wasn't breathing. I panicked! I hit the nurses' button and got no response. I kept talking to my baby, but her skin was darkening in my arms from lack of oxygen. She wasn't breathing!

I struggled to get my legs untangled from the sheets and managed to get out into the hall, holding onto Heidi and screaming as loud as I could manage.

"Somebody help me!"

Nurses appeared from all directions and rushed Heidi into the nursery. By that time she was blue all over, and I watched in horror through the window as they worked to get her breathing again. One of the nurses pulled down the shade on the nursery window so that I didn't have to watch my baby die. Doctors and staff kept running into the nursery. I was near hysteria. Through the PA system I could hear alarms going off and the chant, "Code blue, code blue," followed by the numbers for the nursery. They brought an Isolette and took her away. This was a nightmare.

Nurses came into my room to comfort me. The one in charge put her hands on my shoulders. "The doctors have her breathing again, and they took her down to the NICU," she said, looking me in the eye. "We're lucky because two of the finest pediatric neurologists in the country are visiting the hospital today, and one of them was on duty. He's working on your daughter right now. The best thing you can do is stay calm while they take care of her."

I fought for composure while two other nurses took my shaken roommate out to the hall. Throughout the rest of the day and night, doctors were in and out with questions about family history as well as updates on Heidi's tests and her condition. They would not let me see her because of the continuous testing, and she still was having breath-holding seizures. Her father arrived in the evening, and after I filled him in on what had occurred, we worked through the night recounting family history on a variety of forms. Periodically, we called our mothers to ask questions about the health history of older generations of our families.

I barely slept. What-ifs and questions tormented me. My husband was asleep on the bed next to mine, and I was awake and scared. The quiet in the corridors was oppressive.

Suddenly, Dad was there in my hospital room. He moved over and held me, rocking me back and forth. He said, "She's going to live. I know you're frightened, but she is tough and she's going to be fine."

He gave me another long hug and disappeared into the wall. I stayed still so that I could hold onto the feeling of his comfort for as long as possible.

It wasn't until the third day of Heidi's life that the doctors diagnosed the problem. They told me she had been injured by the difficult birth, and droplets of blood on the surface of her brain had caused the seizures. They had started her on anti-seizure medication and she had not had an episode for almost 12 hours. They felt it was now safe for me to visit her.

When I walked into the NICU, I found her Isolette surrounded by nurses and doctors. I had had to scrub up and don a gown before I could see her. Next to the preemies surrounding her in the NICU, Heidi looked like a giant baby. She lay on her side, one little fist tucked under her cheek and the other arm draped over her hip like a starlet in a 1940s photo. The staff referred to her as Miss Heidi because of her stylish pose.

I longed to hold my baby in my arms. The nurse brought me a chair and showed me how to put my hands through the little portholes so that I could touch her. She was attached to tubes, including an oxygen supply. I didn't know where to touch that wouldn't hurt her. The nurse showed me that I could stroke her arm, leg, and cheek. The minute I touched Heidi's soft little cheek, I saw her relax.

Seeing the baby's composure change, the nurse declared, "She knows her mommy."

I visited her whenever I wanted to, no matter the time of day or night. After a few of my visits, the staff began to notice that minutes before I arrived on the unit, Heidi's heart would begin to race. Their checks found her fine, just excited, and they became convinced that she could sense me coming. I did not feel up to explaining why my apparently psychic daughter knew that her psychic mother was about to enter the room. I just enjoyed knowing that she recognized my thoughts, and that we already had formed a wonderful bond. By four days after Heidi's birth, all the tests showed she was a normal, healthy baby, and that when the blood droplets were reabsorbed, she would be fine. I was overjoyed to have a little daughter to go with my two wonderful sons.

My mother, Blake, and Travis visited as I sat in a wheelchair inside the NICU and held Heidi in my arms. The three of them looked at us through a glass wall.

Blake showed how excited he was by careening around the hallway. Travis had a sour look on his face, and I could tell he was having a hard time with the appearance of a baby sister. It certainly didn't help that Mommy was still in the hospital.

Back in my room that night, I was dozing while trying to watch the news on TV when I heard Dad's whistle and saw him walk in the open door of my hospital room. His face bore a satisfied smile, just like the day at my house when he had held Blake for the first time.

"She's a keeper, Nancy," he said happily, "and a born fighter. She will get through this and much more and keep on going. She looks just like you did when you were born, a real beauty!"

He sat down on the side of my bed and hugged me. Without my telling him, he knew my concerns about the boys' reaction to having a baby sister around. His tone was confident as he said, "Blake will take over with her just like he did with Travis, and Travis will be jealous but protective of her as well. You have an uneven number of kids now, so there will be scrapping!" He stood, leaned down to kiss my forehead, and was gone.

If Dad said she would survive, then she would. I knew it. He had never lied to me about anything. I finally felt that I no longer guarded her, but was actually mothering her. I allowed myself to enjoy having had a pregnancy that had gone full term. What an utter miracle Heidi's life was!

I was especially grateful for her survival when my doctor told me the pathology testing showed that the placenta contained evidence that Heidi had a twin that did not make it. I grieved for that loss, but I focused on the realization that my daughter was going to come home and live with us and meet her rough-and-tumble brothers.

Mother visited the next day while the boys were in school and we sat together celebrating my success. She said, "Heidi looks exactly like you did when you were born! It took my breath away when we peeked through the recovery room door, and I saw you holding—you. Except for the blue eyes. They won't be brown like yours."

I knew Heidi was going to have blue eyes because that's what I had dreamt about since long before I got pregnant with her. Whenever I visualized her as a little girl, I could see her eyes were the same blue as the eyes of so many members of Dad's family. Even though I hadn't given birth to Blake and Travis, when I had been getting ready to adopt each of them, I had dreamt about their eyes too.

It was finally real to me that Heidi was going to live. After all the setbacks—the miscarriages, the difficult pregnancy and birth, and then Heidi's seizures—it seemed impossible, but it was happening.

They released me before it was safe for Heidi to come home, and my friend Marty, who was also my neighbor, picked me up and drove me to the hospital for the next few days so that I could hold Heidi and breastfeed her. I hated leaving Heidi at the hospital alone. I knew she would feel my absence, but she also was aware when I was coming because the staff would see her heart rate rise and in minutes I would arrive. She was picking me up at about the time I left home to come see her. Part of me was happy that she seemed to have inherited my psychic abilities and part was not because I knew that these abilities had their ups and downs.

Finally, the doctors told me that Heidi would be released the next day. She was two weeks old. I was holding her and rocking her when they told me, and on some level she understood because her heart monitor signaled the rising rate of her heartbeat.

"There she goes, getting excited again," her nurse said. "She's ready to go home too."

I called my husband to let him know that we could bring the baby home the next day, but he was monitoring exams for his college courses. That night I was talking on the phone with my friend Kitty about it. I had consulted with her husband Carl, a Delaware State Trooper and head of the Sherlock Squad, on some cold cases. Carl overheard Kitty's end of our conversation and said, "Tell Nancy we'll come pick them up with the rest of the guys from the squad. We want to meet this baby." I had been working with the cold case squad for several years, and they were all happy to do me a favor. Thank goodness for such generous neighbors. They had even helped out with taking care of the boys part of the time when Mother had to go back to work.

The pediatrician wouldn't release Heidi until I got instructions on how to care for her in case the seizures happened again. She had not had a seizure for days, but the possibility remained. The prospect of being the person responsible for her care—with no doctors and nurses within reach—was frightening, but I shook off the negative thoughts. I had been afraid for too long and now I needed to start enjoying her.

I dressed Heidi in her going-home outfit, little pajamas that zipped up the front and a pale yellow snowsuit. The troopers were downstairs waiting as the nurses brought us down in a wheelchair. For her first introduction to my friends, Heidi was sound asleep.

The guys had cameras and were excited to see this long-anticipated baby. "She's a pip," said Carl of the cold case squad. Carl had given me the nickname "Lady Sherlock" because of my accurate work with his team. The rest of the guys agreed with Carl's assessment of Heidi as they bundled us into the police car, and then they jumped into their squad cars to escort us home.

Heidi slept the whole way thanks to my insistence that they not turn on the sirens. When we got to my house, the troopers gave me a beautiful plant in a macramé hanger and a stuffed toy for Heidi. I carried her into the house and laid her in the little crib waiting for her in the living room.

The doctors gave strict instructions to keep her near me in case she had another seizure so that I could get her breathing again.

After the troopers left I sat rigidly in a recliner across from the crib and watched Heidi breathe until the steady rhythm calmed me. It had been a terrifying two weeks. Gradually, I relaxed, reminding myself that the doctors had made it clear that the droplets of blood would probably be reabsorbed within six months, and then they would wean her off the seizure medication. Once this part of it was over, they expected her to be just fine. I watched her sleep, enjoying the first quiet moments alone. Shortly, I heard the excited voices of the boys arriving home from school and started to get up to waylay them at the door and order quiet.

Blake burst through the door first shouting, "She's here, she's here! I told you she would be here!"

I had heard him hollering as he crossed the yard but I was not fast enough to get to the door. I was afraid Blake's enthusiasm might cause a disaster as it so often did, but Heidi remained sound asleep through all the noise and activity. Either she had been knocked out by the seizure medicine, or she was one relaxed baby.

I watched Travis come scowling in the door. He walked over to the crib and stood there glaring at Heidi. "Is she going to die, Mom?" he asked with the bluntness of a five year old.

I assured him that she was *not* going to die. He continued to glare at her with a stormy face. Blake was talking a mile a minute, and Heidi finally opened her eyes.

"Look, she's awake," crowed Blake. "Hi, baby!"

She gave the boys a serious stare as I swept her up for a diaper change and feeding. They followed me into her room and examined every inch of her and she lay there silently, studying her brothers and the room around her. Finally, she had had enough poking and prodding. Hunger took over and she started to holler.

Her brothers loved that. "Wow," said Travis holding his ears. "She's kinda loud. Can you tell her to use her inside voice?"

I laughed. "I'm sorry, buddy, but babies don't have inside voices.

They're supposed to be loud so you know when they need something."

Blake crowed, "My baby is the loudest baby ever."

"That's because you don't remember how loud *you* were," I told him. It was nice to share her with my boys and to see how all three reacted. She followed their every move even when she was hollering.

Travis returned to the living room to watch me nurse Heidi. He was wearing ear muffs. I struggled not to laugh at his solution to her bellowing. He said, "Mom, can we go outside and tell everyone she's finally here?"

Just minutes after they had gone outside into the January cold, Blake flung open the door, blasting us with cold air. "Can we show the kids our sister, Mom?"

The best I could do was let them see her through the storm door. Their friends gathered outside the frosted glass, and Blake directed the procession to make sure everyone had a turn. I could hear Travis bragging about how loud Heidi cried, and the little kids all agreed she was tiny and kind of red in the face.

After they were through showing off their little sister, the boys came inside for hot chocolate. A knock at the door gave away a surprise I had for the boys but hadn't told them about yet. My mother was coming to visit and help me out over the weekend. Blake ran to the door and started to scream in delight, "Guppy's here! Travis, come see!"

As Mother hustled in the door to keep the cold from hitting the baby, I saw my dad standing behind her smiling broadly. I wished that he could have lived to play with all three of my children. He would have been such a wonderful grandfather to them. Dad waved and smiled, and I felt his love pour into me.

Mother turned around suddenly and stared right at him. Later, after the boys were in bed, she said, "He came in with me, didn't he?"

"Yes," I answered, "he was right behind you."

Mom said, "I turned around because I thought I felt his arm on my shoulder. I'm glad he's here to see your kids. They are such great kids. And Heidi is home at last." We sat in my living room, watching this little miracle. Heidi had the funniest habit of twirling her foot while she nursed. No matter how well wrapped she was, that little twirling foot undid the blankets.

We continued to sit there in the quiet. Heidi had been a long time in the growing, but she was so beautiful. Mother and I were both smiling to ourselves as Dad sat in a chair across from us, watching and smiling too.

Chapter 13

The Boy by the Railroad Tracks

Heidi was doing well, and I grew used to having a baby around while dealing with two busy boys.

Unfortunately, elsewhere, things weren't so good. A child was missing, and Carl, head of the Sherlock Squad, called to see if I was up to helping out on this one. A seven-year-old boy—the same age as Blake—was riding his bike home from school when he was taken. Two neighbors saw the kidnapping and called the Delaware State Police right away. Despite the rapid response, there was no sign of this child. Carl hoped my skills would help them find the boy quickly before he was harmed.

Carl and several other officers came to my house after my kids were in bed. They brought photos of the little boy and some of his favorite toys as well as maps of the area. I looked through the photos and my heart sank. I knew at once it was too late. Being used to how I worked after several years together, the troopers watched my face.

"He's dead, isn't he?" Carl asked, sounding tired and discouraged.

"I'm afraid so," I said. "But we shouldn't assume that I'm right. Let's start from square one." I shuffled through the photos again, and as I did I kept seeing the little fellow's body dumped beside a railroad track. He looked so pale and helpless lying there that it was hard for me to concentrate and keep my distance emotionally from what I was seeing. Unpleasant images flooded my mind, and I struggled to keep my composure.

Early in my career as a psychic detective, it had been nearly impossible to keep information like this at a safe enough distance for me to get what the police needed without losing myself in a victim's horror. It had been a constant battle within my mind to find the balance I needed to do the job without succumbing to the pain and terror embedded in the victim's memory. I learned to visualize myself standing *beside* the victim, and to use only his or her thought patterns to get the images started and then to quickly separate myself from those thoughts so that I would be less affected by the horror of what the person went through.

The real trick, which I learned over time, was to get that mess under control as fast as I could so that I could distance myself emotionally. With more distance I was able to give detailed descriptions of what happened in each case and what the perpetrator looked like.

I interpreted the images in my mind: "I feel his fear as a man grabs him. There are two men in a pickup truck. The boy doesn't know either of them. They quickly tape him up and throw him in the bed of the truck and take off. I can hear the men talking, but I can't tell what they're saying."

"Can you tell which way they went?" one of the troopers asked.

I brought the image back into my mind. "They pass a gas station on the left that also sells snacks and such. They are flying when they pass that station—moving very fast. They know that some people have seen them. They travel about a half mile past that gas station and turn onto a bigger road, four-lane, heading south. It looks like it might be Route 13, heading southeast into the Delaware City area."

"Are you sure it's not Route 8?" Carl asked.

"I don't think so because 8 is swampy along that area and 13 is not," I said. "I think it's 13. This road has four lanes."

I stopped to refocus and then described to the troopers what I saw. The truck turned down a one-lane, bumpy side road. If it was paved at all, it was rutted, and the poor child was being thrown around in the back of the truck. He was crying, and he knew he wasn't going to make it if he couldn't get away, but his feet and hands were taped together.

I saw the truck slow down as it came up on a dilapidated farm house. The house was so old the paint was long gone. It looked gray, but I thought it was probably white originally. To the right of that house was a broken-backed structure with a huge hole in the roof where it had collapsed. Remains of old red paint were visible on the sides, and the old barn door was hanging loose on its hinges.

It was getting dark as they unloaded the child, but I couldn't see any lights. They carried him into the broken-down house. The front door wasn't even locked. The men moved the child to a back room next to what was once a kitchen—I could see an old rusted stove there and some cabinets half hanging off the wall.

I told the officers, "I can see a broken metal bed, barely standing, in that back room. The men threw the child on that bed." I took a deep breath, and as I did I felt my father's hand on my shoulder.

I steadied myself and then forced out the words. "They untaped him and then they took turns raping him and beating him until he died."

I stopped to rest. This was the most brutal thing I had ever visualized. The troopers waited silently for me to start again as I felt the continued steady pressure of my father's hand.

"After the boy dies," I said, "they argue over where to dump his body. The older man wants to dump him in a landfill, but the younger one wants to put him somewhere where his remains can be found. He feels guilty about what he did and if you get to question them, he will tell you what happened. The older man is the younger one's father, and he has no feelings at all. The younger one is doing what his father wants because he is terribly afraid of his father. The young one volunteers to get rid of the body so that he can put it where it can be found.

"The next image I see is that of the child's body so close to busy railroad tracks that I'm afraid the rush of the air from the passing train will pull the body under it. I can feel an engineer peering at the body from a distance trying to figure out what it is. As the train roars by it, he sees that it's the body of a young boy, and he reports it on the radio. The body was dumped at night, and the engineer sees it just after dawn. God, I hope I'm wrong, but the images are so strong and they never waver, so I think that they are correct."

They asked me for some more detail and for descriptions of the perpetrators. I gave them everything that I could range on the two men who did this. Inside I was feeling sick, and my chest hurt. I felt like I had absorbed some of the terrible beating this youngster took. I was sure that I could never be so close to a crime like this again. I was not cut out for such horrors.

After the troopers left, I sat in the darkened living room for some time, thinking that this was not work that I could handle, not if I wanted to hold onto my sanity.

My father appeared across the room, sitting opposite me. He said, "You have to learn to stand *beside* the victim, but keep yourself out of the victim's thoughts."

I said, "I know that, Dad, but it's not easy to do, especially with a case involving a child. He was Blake's age, and those men were monsters."

"You've been given a gift that you need to honor, Nancy. Do you know how few people have the abilities you have?" His voice was full of conviction. "You can help to stop *killers*, and I know you will find a way to survive."

"Right now it feels too hard to cope with," I told him. "I can't get the child's screams out of my head. I had to watch him die, and I couldn't stop it."

He said, "Your work will one day help to prevent killings as you learn to do it better. But you have to get used to those terrible images and learn how to survive seeing them. Learn to cleanse your mind of the work when you are done and then go back to your life. That's what the police learn to do, and so can you."

I nodded mutely and sat there in a daze with those nightmarish images repeating.

I fell asleep that night with the child's screams echoing in my mind. I had nightmares about it all night and woke up exhausted. How on earth could I learn to keep enough distance? As sensitive as I was, it was incomprehensible to me that to do this work I had to immerse myself in the ugliest human behavior possible. It was the Nazis all over again.

All day I felt overwhelmed with sadness. The little boy's parents were waiting to hear that he was all right, but instead they would bury him. I was going to have to figure out if I could learn to withstand this kind of stress. By nature, I wanted to help people, and I could already see that my work could help the police. But what was it going to do to *me*? Could I stay balanced within myself? Or would the horror overwhelm me?

"You can do this, Nance," Dad had said. "You're strong enough to withstand it."

Something he said in one of our conversations about the Light of Life nagged at me for quite a while. He had told me that love in the world increased the Light of Life; I wondered, did wars, anger, murders, and hatred diminish it? Was this the proverbial fight between good and evil?

He sent me images of mothers loving their babies and fathers guiding their children. Juxtaposed were other pictures he sent of murder and mayhem. It seemed to me that the loving images sustained a stronger light around them, but I was not sure if I had that right. I sensed that there was something more that I was not comprehending.

I recalled a time not long after Dad's death, when Blake was just a toddler. We had stopped at a small playground, my goal being to keep Blake occupied and to wear him out so he would sleep better that night. I saw Dad watching his grandson. Suddenly Blake turned and saw his grandfather and ran to him to get a hug. My father was able to lift his grandson high off the ground. Ripples of giggles filled the air as my Dad flew Blake around. Then he set the boy down beside me, kissed my cheek, and walked away into a grove of trees.

I felt a strong tug on the hem of my shorts. I looked down to an excited Blake pointing at the trees: "Dat my dampa! Right?"

"Yes, that is your grandpa." I ruffled his hair as he dragged me back to the biggest slide at the playground. He was too young to understand what a ghost was. Dad's appearance was natural to him. The love and joy they experienced for those few minutes transcended the boundaries of life and death. With that memory still vivid in my mind, I heard Dad's voice in my head. "Yes, you see it now, Nancy. That kind of love cannot be diminished by evil. It is more powerful than any evil."

Carl called me the next morning to tell me that a railroad engineer on a run had called his boss to report the body of a child dumped beside a railroad track. I was stunned. As much as this case had hurt me, I had been incredibly exact.

The medical examiner's determination as to the time of death confirmed that the little boy was dead when I did my reading. He died of internal injuries from a beating and asphyxia. He had been sexually assaulted by two men. I took no pleasure in being right, but it helped me to understand the value of my work. It was important to me to be accurate enough not to waste the time of busy detectives. Measuring my own correctness was a part of how I gauged my usefulness to police departments. Clearly, I was getting things right, so the big question was whether could I handle these horrible images, separate myself from them, and lead as normal a life as a psychic person could.

Chapter 14
Grandpa

One morning seven months after we had brought Heidi home, the sun shone in my kitchen windows as I washed dishes. With the window open I could hear laughter from my neighbor's yard. My neighbor's father played with his grandkids and several of their friends, including my boys. Heidi was asleep in her room. She no longer suffered seizures and had been weaned from the medication that helped to control them.

Suddenly, I heard the little girl next door exclaim, "Now that your Mom has a *real* baby she borned, she's going to throw you in the trash. She won't want adopted kids any more. And you leave my grandpap alone. You don't even have any grandpap, do ya?"

I froze, horrified.

Blake, full of hurt and rage, hauled off and hit her, knocking her down. I ran for the back door and across the yard as the little girl's grandfather rescued her from my enraged son. The grandfather took the girl to task for her hurtful comments. I jumped the fence and got ahold of Blake. I insisted that he apologize for striking the girl. Travis ran up the backyard and straight into the house. Blake stormed in after him and I followed them both. Travis sat on the couch, arms folded across his little heaving chest. He was hurt and furious, and I sat down so he could fold himself into my lap. He sat there sobbing.

"I hate that girl," said Blake. "I'm gonna rip her head off. Did you hear what she said, Mom?" Blake piled into my lap and I held them both.

"Yes I heard," I said. "It was cruel of her to say that, and it's not true. She's little so she has no idea what she is talking about. You're all my treasures. All three of you are my special babies. I don't care how you came to be mine, just that all of you are mine. With you guys, I got to choose you. That's really special, and when you have a baby born to you when you least expect it, well, that's special too."

"Yeah, but what about our grandpaps?" Travis sobbed.

I explained to him that their grandfathers had died, that my father met Blake, but he never got to meet Travis.

"If they had lived they both would have loved you so much," I said. "My dad would have taken you fishing and taught you how to build stuff. He has missed so much by not knowing you, but I know he watches out for you from where he is now."

"Are you sure?" Blake said.

"I am sure, son. Quite sure."

Both boys claimed that it wasn't the same as having a real grandpa.

"No, it isn't," I admitted. "Just remember that I love you lots and lots and that's what's important. And being born or adopted does not make a bit of difference to me. I'm still going to hug you both until you pop."

"Mom, you're squishing me," laughed Travis.

"You hug too hard, Mom," Blake giggled. He couldn't sit still for long and squirmed off the couch and ran up to his room where he began to bang around. It would take him a while to calm down from today's wounding at the hands of the neighbor girl.

Travis and I snuggled for a while. "Mom, are you sure you don't like that baby better'n me?" Travis glared in the direction of his baby sister's room.

"How could I like her better than you? I have to do so much work to take care of her. You guys are bigger and a lot more fun and you don't make poopy diapers."

This satisfied Travis and he hopped down and went back outside to play in our sandbox. It was then I noticed Blake's voice in deep conversation. I crept upstairs to make sure he wasn't getting into mischief.

I peeked into the boys' room. "Them cows gots four stomachs? What do they need all those stomachs for?" I saw Blake pause and study the air beside him.

My father looked up at me, smiled, and winked. I backed out of Blake's sight and listened to the conversation.

Blake laughed. "Well," he said, "I always thought the cows were chewing gum. Here it's chewed up grass. Yuck. What do you mean a cow with a window in her side?"

I hurried back downstairs to my chair. I had a hunch I knew what was coming next.

Blake's feet hit the floor in turbo mode. "Mom, I do have a grandpa! He was just in my bedroom. He told me all about cows and they have four stomachs. Did you know that?" He paused to breathe and see if I believed him. I nodded.

"He says to tell you to take us to see the cow with the window in her stomach. He said you'd know what he was talking about. Do you?"

"Yes, I do. At the experimental farm at the University of Delaware, they have a cow with a porthole in her stomach so you can see how her digestion works."

"Can we go see it?" he begged.

"I'll call and find out."

He slammed out the back door and promptly fell off the back step in his excitement to share the big news with Travis. "Mom's going to take us to see a cow with a window in its stomach! Our grandpa came and told me all about it!"

"He can't come here, Blake," said Travis, who seemed embarrassed for his brother's mistake. "He's dead."

"I know, but he was just here. You can ask Mom."

The door opened and Mr. Serious looked at me: "Mom, Blake is telling tales again."

"Well, this time he's not, son. I can't explain how it works, but your grandfather was just here. I saw him sitting on the bed next to Blake."

"See, I told you," Blake said.

Travis' mouth fell open. "For real?"

I assured him, yes, for real. "See?" said Blake, "We do have a grandpa. He said he watches us all the time and he loves us a lot." Blake hugged his little brother. "He wanted me to hug you for him. And then you hug me for him."

Travis reached his little arms around his big brother and gave him a good hug.

"See, now that girl there can say what she wants," Blake said. "We have a grandpa who loves us. It's just that he's a ghost and can't be here all the time. Just sometimes. Special occasions. Right, Mom?"

"Right," I said. But I had a problem to deal with. "Now boys, other people won't understand this, so this will be our special secret, okay?"

Blake nodded. "That's what Grandpa told me, Mom. I know."

Blake charged out the back door heading straight for the neighbor girl. "We're going to see a cow with a window in its side," he bellowed, "and you're not invited because you were mean. And, my mom chose us special. Not just an accident of being born like you, poopyhead."

His little nemesis headed into her house wailing, "Blake said he was chosen and I was just an accident!" I knew my phone would be ringing from that one.

By now Heidi was sitting up, crawling, and playing with toys. Her favorite game was tossing toys out of the playpen and waiting for her brothers to retrieve them for her. They loved doing it because they liked the fact that she was interacting with them. Eventually, they'd get bored and Heidi would go back to entertaining herself.

"Mom, you gotta come see what Heidi's doing," Blake said one morning.

"Hurry up, Mom, she's doing something weird with her ball," Travis said.

I walked around the wall of the kitchen into the living room to see Heidi, sporting a toothless grin, sitting up with her favorite crocheted ball in her hands. She put the ball down and pushed it away so hard I knew it would end up out of her reach. As the ball started to roll too far, it quivered and slowly stopped rolling.

Heidi glared at the ball until it started quivering again, and then it slowly rolled right back to her hands. She picked up the ball, waved it at me, and gave me a big smile. It was clear that she knew what she was doing. She put down the ball and repeated the entire sequence exactly the way she'd just done it, including waving the ball at me and smiling. My daughter was telekinetic.

Chapter 15
Mind Wide Open

By the time Heidi was two years old, my marriage had ended and I was raising the children on my own. Working as a psychic was now my full-time job, and I had a great deal of success with both personal readings and police work. When I cracked a case, the detectives I worked with would share the story of my success with other police departments. My reputation was spreading, and I had mixed feelings about this fact. The personal pressures accompanying my divorce made police work stressful, but I needed to support my children and I had to put aside my difficulties and develop this new and unusual career.

I had always been fascinated by mystery stories, and now I had the chance to work on them directly. The more cases I worked, the better able I was to figure out how to improve my accuracy and to handle the negative images I had to wade through in my mind. My problem was that I lacked confidence that my efforts were useful to the police. I was painfully aware of how important it was that I not waste their time, and I was always afraid that tracking down my clues would send them on wild goose chases. Col. Irvin Smith of the Delaware State Police continued to insist the results were quite accurate and encouraged me to keep going.

As the number of cases mounted, I couldn't really argue with the outcomes. At best, my results were 90 percent accurate. That didn't mean I solved 90 percent of the cases; rather it indicated that 90 percent of the time I gave clues to law enforcement that turned out to be useful and accurate. One of the officers told me that because I was brought in on the toughest cases, my work, on average, saved six months of investigative time. That simple statistic helped me to realize the value of my skills.

My reputation as a person capable of assisting the police in solving crimes had spread all over the tri-state area: Delaware, Maryland, and Eastern Pennsylvania. I was living in Newark, Delaware at that time. I had never realized what an effective gossip system existed within law enforcement. I was often invited to speak before police training organizations, such as the local chapter of Harvard Associates in Police Science in Wilmington, Delaware, and a local meeting of the FBI National Academy in Dover. I trained law enforcement officials on how to tell when a psychic was real—and how to get the most out of working with a psychic when they did find the real thing. I was also giving seminars for the general public in conjunction with a local college that had invited me to teach in their continuing education department.

It was becoming routine for psychic individuals to come up to me after my speeches to share their experiences with me. They would often try to show me they were "real" by revealing something that would come up in these situations almost without exception.

The conversation would begin, "I saw a man standing behind you— over your right shoulder. He looks a lot like you." I would ask for specifics. "He's very tall, and he has black hair with a little gray on the sides. He has a big grin and he's doing something funny."

The man, of course, was Dad. He and I had agreed on a specific signal so that I would know that an intuitive person really had seen him.

"Thank you for telling me," I would say. "It was nice of you to make the gesture." Such discussions then moved to the person's budding psychic ability and how he or she could learn to use it—and to live with it.

The first time this happened, about five years after Dad's death, I realized that my father was bringing me proof of his existence in a way that was independent of my own thoughts. At a time when I struggled to cope with the pressures in my personal life and my growing psychic skills, these occurrences banished any lingering doubts that my interactions with him were real.

As a psychic, I have had many conversations with my clients about their experiences with relatives who have come back to comfort them; it's more common than I ever would have guessed. The veil between life and death is not as rigid as general belief systems would have us imagine. I have been comforted by knowing that others experience sightings too; in my case, my visits with my father have come more easily and more frequently. My discussions with others who have seen their loved ones affirm in my mind that departed souls are making an attempt to let the living know that existence continues after death and to bring comfort to those left behind, giving new meaning to the word love.

As noted, Dad has turned up many times as I work murder cases, helping me to cope with the violence in the images as they flood through me, and with the nausea those images produce. At such times I have always been grateful for the steadying force of his hand on my shoulder. As his healing energy flows through me, the nausea eases, and I am better able to focus on images that detectives need to solve their cases—without the embarrassment of throwing up.

On one occasion in Wilmington, Detectives Leroy Landon and Jay Ingraham—with whom I had worked many cases—were driving me through a neighborhood. Detective Tony Rispoli was also in the car with us. I had just finished doing a reading on a site where a dead body had been shoved under the sidewalk on a lot that was scheduled to be loaded with fill. Just before the fill was brought in, a scavenger had found the body and called the police. But for his call, the body probably never would have been found.

The case seemed strange to begin with because I connected the body to another murder I had worked before—a woman who had been followed home from a grocery store by three black men who raped her and then murdered her with a knife. The style of these two murders was completely different so the likelihood of it being the same set of killers, with two completely different M.O.s, was remote.

I insisted that the man whose body was found under the sidewalk, who also happened to be black, was killed by the same three men who killed the white woman on the other side of Wilmington. Two different types of victims, one male and one female, two different ethnicities, and two different types of neighborhoods. This defied the training of the three detectives, and we were discussing that it seemed unlikely to be the same killers as we drove back to headquarters. Suddenly I found myself inside the thought patterns of one of the killers. I gagged, ready to lose my dinner.

Det. Landon slammed on the brakes and pulled over. I jumped out of the squad car and tried to let the cool evening air help me ward off the nausea. Instead, it grew worse. I jumped back in the car and said, "Get me out of here!" Leroy Landon knew me well enough to understand that I was too close to something so he drove to the next block where I could calm down and tell them what was happening.

"Right now," I told them, "the killer is in the house where you just stopped! It made me sick because he was drunk and his mind was wide open, and I could pick up images of the two murders as he was thinking about them. He was savoring the memories of the murders and bragging to someone about both of them." I pointed out the house and the room on the second floor where this man was located at the time.

We were truly lucky that night because the police were in the middle of a house-to-house search on that block just as I pointed out the room he was in. Landon ran around the block and joined the search so that he could find out who was in that room. He wrote down the names of everyone in the house at the time. I told the detectives, "The killer is in the rear right-hand room on the second floor of that house." Detectives Ingraham and Rispoli waited with me while Leroy ran back into the midst of the search.

At the station, we referenced the list of occupants in that house and the detectives put together six photos in a lineup for me to look at. Could I pick out the killer? I pointed at the man whose head I had entered—and he had been found in the upstairs back bedroom of the house I had picked out. The detectives knew this man and those he usually hung out with, so they quickly put together another photo lineup, and I picked out the other two suspects right away. I even told them what to do to get one of the three suspects to turn on the other two, and that he would provide descriptions of the two killings while claiming that he was just a lookout and did not kill the victims. I also told the police that this wasn't true; he was the killer.

The information I provided helped them get the suspect to talk, and we solved two very different murders at the same time. Two different killings—and my illogical conclusion that they were connected turned out to be correct. To this day Detectives Landon, Ingraham, and Rispoli claim that I threw up in their squad car. I maintain that I *almost* did but managed not to.

I succeeded in helping to solve many such cases, but I loathed the evil, brutal images I had to sort through to get the needed information. I hoped that I would get stronger and better able to handle the revulsion as time went on. In the meantime, my father's extra energy and the comfort of his hand made the whole mess more tolerable, although he was not there the night I ran into the killer's thought patterns. I wondered if that might have been because it happened so fast that Dad couldn't react.

The 90 percent accuracy of my information meant that 10 percent of the time, I was inaccurate. When I made mistakes, I would analyze what happened to figure out where I had gone wrong. Often I would find that my emotions got in the way.

Once when I had gone out with Delaware State Police detectives, one of them remarked that the victim, who had survived but was so badly injured he was curled up in a ball and unable to speak or communicate in any way, showed fear of the black male orderlies on the hospital unit where he was recovering. I felt uncomfortable about the way he said that, thinking it might be coming from his own prejudices rather than the fact that it might connect to the case. I believe that my discomfort with his comment and my misinterpretation of what he said made me shy away from the reality that the assailant was in fact an African American. I sat with a police artist and described the attacker accurately, in fact; I thought he was a

Latino rather than an African-American male, as his skin seemed more light than dark to me. When the police found the man using that drawing, the people who knew him made the same comment: it looked like the suspect except that the skin color was too light. My emotional reaction to the detective's comment had thrown me off. It was a learning experience that made me take extra care later.

My father often helped to steady me so I could work more effectively. He was doing it now from the other side just as he had throughout my life, even as a child. I remembered once, not long after we arrived in Chile when I was six or seven years old, I had come down with some illness and ran a dangerously high fever. The doctor came to our house and checked me over. Mother and Dad still didn't speak Spanish well, so I translated what the doctor said.

"He says my fever is too high and he has to take a blood sample," I relayed. Then I thought about what I had just said and grew frightened. "What does that mean?" The doctor took a needle out of his bag and came at me with it. To me it looked as big as the needles my father used on cows to cure bloat. I was out of the bed and airborne into my father's arms. He sat down in the nearest chair and held me, and calmed me down.

Dad said, "He has to take some blood from your arm so he can send it away to be tested."

"With that big needle?" I screeched. "It will go right through my arm and come out the other side."

Dad hugged me and then he held my face between his hands. He said, "You have to be very brave. A lot of children are sick here in Chillán, and they thought it was just the flu but it isn't. Your fever is way too high, so they think it is something much more serious. You give your blood to the doctor, and you will help all the other kids get better too."

I was not buying it, but it was obvious I must have this test. My fear of needles, due to all the vaccinations required every time we went overseas, was enormous. As Dad held me in his lap and held my arm out toward the doctor's awful needle, I felt this sudden energy flow from him and through me. The energy made the fear stop, and I was able to hold still and tolerate the blood being drawn.

The test results showed I had typhoid fever. I saw and felt the fear in my parents, but Dad put his arms around Mother, and I watched him take her fear away. As a child, I had wondered how he did that; as an adult engaged in my unusual profession, I still do not fully understand it. I just know that his touch has enabled me to give speeches and work cases without panicking. Over time, I haven't needed that strong touch as much, but I often think of the feel of his hand on my shoulder, over and over again, as I face my fears.

Chapter 16
Zip-a-Dee-Doo-Dah

After my divorce in the late 1970s, Mother and I purchased a large home in Newark, Delaware, and moved in together. We both needed some moral support, and the children were shuttling back and forth for visits with their father, who lived on the other side of the city. Living in two households presented problems for the kids as their father and I set different house rules. Blake in particular acted up after the visits, and his behavior was a lot to handle. Mother was a wonderful stabilizing force for the children, and she enjoyed the companionship, although I am sure that there were times when the noise and enthusiasm of the children, who were now 10, 9, and 4, were too much for her.

My business as a psychic consultant was thriving, with most of my work involving helping people deal with the stresses of life. Most of my clients were people trying to find jobs, or get better jobs; some of them wanted to find life partners, and there was an increasing number who wanted my help in solving burglaries. I needed the income to take care of my children financially. To help care for the kids' emotional needs, Mother and I filled the house with as much positive energy as we could.

Tired from a long day of work and the uproar of the kids, I sat at the kitchen table with Mother as we snuck some cookies and milk. The boys were outside riding bikes with their friends, and Heidi was busy in her room upstairs. She had announced that she was going to clean her room by herself, which was a four year old's idea of what a big girl should do. She did not choose to clean it often, but when Mother and I took on the task, she objected with great vigor—wailing and throwing herself on the floor kicking. Heidi was quite theatrical when she chose to be, which led to our new phrase: "Drama, drama, drama." We were careful not to let Heidi hear us say it, as that would set off yet another fit of fury.

Her efforts at cleaning her room usually led to hilarious results. Her favorite toy at the time was a red plastic shovel. She would use it to push mounds of toys across the room and into the closet or under her bed. She preferred the shovel method to any other way we might suggest for putting the toys back where they belonged because her idea of a clean room meant no toys on the floor. It didn't matter if they were piled up elsewhere. Heidi would come downstairs and proudly request that Mother and I inspect her room. We wanted to encourage her nascent efforts at cleaning, so we always praised her lavishly for doing such a great job. At the next opportunity, however, Mother and I would put her room back to rights again and brace for the histrionics that would come when Heidi found out we had properly cleaned her room.

Mother and I munched on our cookies in silence, knowing that the next day we would be correcting Heidi's cleaning operation. I could tell that Mom was a little down. Her painting wasn't going well. She seemed off kilter and discouraged.

I finally asked her what was bothering her. She said, "It's been a long time since we've seen your father. I wonder why he hasn't shown up lately."

I realized that she was right; he hadn't made his presence known in quite a while. "I'm sure he's okay—wherever he is. We're probably having a harder time with this than he is."

I always wondered about the pace of existence on the other side. Maybe he wasn't even aware of how much time passed between his visits with us. For his family, however, the uncertainty of a long separation was hard to bear. To ease my mother's pain, I told her about a conversation I had had with Dad's ghost:

"One day I asked Dad a question about his life in the light and how he kept busy. He had never been a sit-still kind of guy, and I imagined that he would remain busy where he was now. He passed images to me of small children dying. I could feel their fear and confusion without their parents, and he showed me how he would hold and comfort them while he led them to family members who had died before. I would not have thought of souls having jobs in the light but that is how he referred to it, as his new job. I knew how calming to frightened children he had been in his life; it was the perfect thing for him to be doing in his afterlife. Maybe that's why we haven't seen him in a bit."

Mother nodded as tears welled up. I ducked into my office next to our eat-in kitchen to grab a tissue box. As I handed her the box I heard singing and whistling upstairs.

Heidi opened her bedroom door and I could hear her lilting voice singing something familiar. Over and over she sang and then tried to whistle a snippet of "Zip-a-Dee-Doo-Dah."

Mother heard it too. She looked at me in shock. "Do you hear that?"

"I certainly do. I don't believe it though. Isn't that Zip-a-Dee-Doo-Dah?"

"It is," said Mother. "I wonder where she learned that song?"

"I don't know—maybe in school? But it's strange that she should happen to sing it right this minute. And she's not changing the words."

Heidi gave us an all-too-familiar rendition of a song from the Disney classic movie from my childhood, *Song of the South*. "Zip-a-dee-doo-dah" was a phrase Mother and I knew well. Whenever my dad was in a really good mood, he whistled that part of the song over and over. It became his signal to the rest of the family that he had arrived home. Since his death, his whistle had become more significant than ever. Whenever I heard those five notes, I knew he was nearby.

Zip-a-dee-doo-dah, zip-a-dee-ay!
My, oh my, what a wonderful day!
Plenty of sunshine heading my way . . .

She hummed the next part as she marched down the stairs. . . . *bluebird on my shoulder . . .* More humming followed as she marched through the kitchen, into my office, back into the front hall, and then into the kitchen again.

Heidi entered the kitchen again, singing Dad's favorite part of the song just as he used to sing it, with the same mistakes that he always made. And she sang it over and over and over, just as he used to do.

She kept belting out the song as she passed through the kitchen and on into my office. She was not varying what she sang one bit, unlike her usual style to make creative changes in lyrics, rarely singing a song the same way twice. Mother and I continued to watch.

"Heidi, who taught you that song?" I asked as she came through the kitchen yet again.

"Guppy's daddy taught me it. He says it's for happy times. He wants me to sing it right now." Off she went to sing another round.

At her age, Heidi thought of all husbands as daddies. But I wanted to be sure we had understood her.

I said loud and clear, motioning to my mom, "Do you mean Guppy's daddy? Or do you mean her husband, who was my daddy?"

She nailed me with a Heidi glare. Hands on hips, annoyed little foot tap-tapping, she said, "I know he was your daddy, and he's Guppy's too. He's dread."

That was about as clear as mud. Did she mean he was dead, or that his name was Fred?

She grabbed my hand and dragged me into my mother's bedroom. Mother followed us. Heidi led us over to my mother's dresser and pointed to a photo of my father as a young man. As far as I knew, none of us had ever told her who that was. "That's Dread. He's Guppy's daddy. Now, are you going to share those cookies you been sneakin'?"

We left my mother to go get some cookies. In the kitchen, Heidi said to me, "He knows Guppy's sad. He said if I sang her that song she would feel better. She's not feeling better. I saw her tears."

"She does feel better," I assured Heidi. "Sometimes, you cry because you are happy. Sometimes, you can be sad and happy at the same time."

Between bites of cookie she said, "He visits me when I play up there by myself. He's nice. You have a nice daddy."

"I do, don't I?"

"Yup. He made me promise to sing that song right, you know. And I did."

Mother reappeared from her bedroom. She said, "Thank you for the song, Heidi. Guppy was sad today, and you and Fred made me feel a lot better."

"See?" said Heidi in satisfaction.

I sat down and said to Mom, "He wanted you to know he heard you."

"He *would* pick that song to sing," she replied.

We shared a happy moment as we thought of all the times we had heard it sung just like that. He could never remember the whole song, or chose not to. I said, "She sounded just like him! He still teases us."

Our laughter filled the kitchen. Heidi had finished her cookies and milk. "He said you would laugh," she said as she headed up the stairs. "I'm gonna tell him he's right."

We both listened as she talked away in her room. She had closed the door so we could not hear anything but muffled words, snatches of that song, and giggles. Lots of giggles.

When I went up to bed that night I took a photo of Dad into Heidi's bedroom and placed it on her dresser. I had wanted her to know him, and now it was clear that she did.

Chapter 17
Clean Up Your Room

Since my divorce, Blake's behavior had become more and more difficult as he acted out and got into bigger trouble than he had before. Travis and Blake shared a room, which was hard for Travis because he was neat by nature, while Blake could turn a room over like a tornado in nothing flat.

Around the time Blake turned 11, he started to exude some kind of odd electrical energy that physically affected things around him. On more than one occasion, he walked through the kitchen and things he hadn't even touched fell off the counter. This was frustrating to both of us. "Mom, did you see that? I didn't do that!" he wailed after some vegetables for the night's dinner suddenly ended up on the floor after he passed nearby.

"I know, son," I told him. "I saw it happen."

"So now you know I'm not lying!" he said. "I've been telling you I wasn't touching the stuff, but you wouldn't believe me. Now do you believe me?"

"I do believe you," I told him, "and I'm sorry I didn't believe you before."

I asked him how often this happened. He told me that at school, books fell off shelves, and the teacher thought the room was haunted. He knew when books were going to fly. "I can feel buzzing inside of me when something bad is about to happen," he explained to me.

My seeing it happen made these events easier for both of us; I thought it fascinating that he could do this, and I wondered how I could help him to stop doing it. I worked to calm him down when he was overstressed and taught him a simple meditation technique that seemed to reduce the energy, so fewer objects went flying. But if he was really excited or upset, chaos often ensued.

Today had not been a good day for Travis. Blake upended the contents of the room while he looked for some toy or other, then left the mess and went off to play. This time it wasn't any electrical energy from Blake that caused the destruction—just him being careless and not very considerate of Travis's joint ownership of the space. I had heard the two of them arguing and was waiting to see if they would settle it themselves. I thought they had, but then I heard the front screen door slam and what sounded like Travis thumping around angrily upstairs. I started to get up to haul Blake to task when I heard Travis's voice, a voice filled not with anger, but with worry. It caught my full attention.

"Mom?" said Travis. "I think Grandpa's in my room." I took the stairs two at a time and rushed into the room to find my dad sitting on the edge of Blake's bed. He was smiling, and he wiggled his ears at us.

Travis giggled. "He's funny."

I wanted to make sure Travis wasn't frightened so I said as matter of factly as possible, "Your grandpa *is* funny, isn't he?" My younger son half hid behind me as he peered out at the stranger.

"Travis, this is your grandfather. His name is Fred, and he likes to play jokes."

"But . . ." Travis began, thinking the obvious: *How can this be?*

Blake's head popped in the door.

"Hi, Grandpa!" he said. "See, Travis? I told you he comes to visit. Now he's visiting you too!"

"Blake, you need to clean up this mess you made," said my father. "Travis shouldn't be picking up the messes you make."

"Okey, dokey," Blake said. As my father disappeared, Blake set to the task of putting back the toys he had junked all over the floor.

Dumbfounded, Travis stared at the now-empty bed. "That was my grandpa?"

"It certainly was," I said.

"How'd he do that? Can all dead people do that?" Travis asked this with his voice flying up the scale.

"Not all dead people can do it," I said. "I know of some other folks who have done it. It isn't real common, but it does happen."

"Isn't it cool?" Blake said.

Travis, deep in thought, stared at the bed, where a depression remained in the quilt where my dad had sat. Travis shook his head. "This is really weird, Mom. It's just weird."

"I know it seems that way son, but he won't hurt you."

"No," said Travis. "I mean—he's a ghost, right?"

"Yes, he is."

"But he comes to visit?" Travis continued, reasoning it out.

"Sometimes he does," I told him.

"Like Casper the friendly ghost," Travis said quite seriously, solving the problem. Blake was old enough to laugh at his brother, and I joined in.

"We got our own Casper, Mom!" Blake said as he finished with the cleanup and bolted for the door. He hollered as he thumped down the stairs, "I'll be out front. Call me when dinner's ready!"

"I'm glad he sat on Blake's bed and not mine," said Travis. He sidled cautiously by the offensive spot on Blake's bed. He wrapped his arms around my legs.

I knelt down. "Think of it this way, Travis. He's like an unusual guardian angel to us. He watches out for all of us. Look, he got Blake to clean up the mess."

Travis looked at the neat room. "Blake doesn't seem to mind when Grandpa tells him what to do—like he does when you do. Why is that?"

"Maybe because Grandpa isn't always here. Or perhaps it's because he's a ghost."

Travis laughed. "It takes a friendly ghost to make him behave."

We both laughed.

My mother entered the room and asked, "What's this I hear about a friendly ghost?"

Travis told Mother all about the visit. "Guppy, you're not going to believe this," he began. He took her hand and led her over to the bed. Pointing at the depression on the quilt, Travis told her how his grandpa made Blake clean up the room.

Mother smiled and remarked how handy it would be to have Grandpa around when Blake misbehaves.

Travis reached out cautiously to touch the quilt. "Grandpa was here to visit *me* this time. He came to help me get Blake to behave. Isn't that nice of him?"

Eyebrows up, she looked at me and I nodded.

Then she nodded too. "I think that's special, Travis," said Guppy. "I'm glad he came to see you. I know how much he loves you, and I wish he had lived to see you and love you as much as I do." She hugged my little curly haired son to her.

Travis looked at her with those big, brown, serious eyes, "That's okay, Guppy. I mean, he must love me a lot to get out of his grave and come all the way over here to make Blake be nice. Don't you think?"

She stifled a chuckle at the way Travis expressed it. He was so solemn.

Suddenly he said, "I'm gonna go play now, before it's too late to go outside." Out he went with his favorite ball in hand.

Back downstairs in the kitchen, Mother and I started to work on dinner. We alternated between laughter and tears as we talked about our serious little Travis.

"He's so direct!" said Mom. "He says so much in one small sentence. The other two take pages to get to the point." She wiped her eyes, and I reached for her and hugged her. Then she said, "I appreciate that he comes back. I do. But it wakes up the hurt all over again."

Missing Dad wasn't as hard for us as it used to be, and the humor of his visits made it easier. "Would you rather he didn't do it?" I asked.

There was a long pause as she considered that, then she said, "No. I'd rather know he still exists somewhere."

While she was deliberating my question, I was thinking about it too. Would it be easier if he didn't come? I came to the same conclusion she did. No, it was better to know that his soul still existed out there and that he still loved us.

Over the years and as my psychic abilities grew, my father and I had learned to communicate in a special way. He had told me once that he could "hear" me—my thoughts—even when his spirit wasn't nearby. That knowledge comforted me. Before Dad's death and after, I had enjoyed sharing with him unique things I saw in the course of living. Now I felt like I could do that anytime; I didn't have to wait for his ghost to appear. I learned to send him images of things I saw and enjoyed—my grandson's smile, a sun-flooded cornfield—that I knew he would appreciate too. I cherished this continued connection to him.

I loved that I could ask him an important question and in time he would send me images that provided an answer. During one of his physical appearances he said, "I enjoy our new way of communicating. It isn't as taxing for me as this physical stuff is, and I love hearing from you. And you are so quick to understand the images I send to you—you always were quick to understand new concepts."

It was all so comforting in its own odd way. His visits and our communication forced me to think about death and what it actually entailed. If the soul of a loved one could come back, then, obviously, the two worlds we inhabited coexisted in some wonderful way. Otherwise, how could he do this?

Chapter 18

Out of the Corner

A few months after Dad's visit to Travis, I took the children to the roller rink. With us was Brian, a 16 year old who helped me out with lawn care and house repairs. We roller-skated all afternoon. What a blast! It was years since I had skated, but I hadn't lost my skills. When I started to tire and got off the rink, the kids surrounded me.

"Mom, we're hungry," Blake said. He and Travis were growing so quickly that they were perpetually hungry. Bottomless, in fact.

"Well, we can't eat a lot, but we can get sodas and snacks."

We rolled into the snack bar. I settled them at a table with their food and then rolled toward the counter to get napkins. I didn't see a large scooped out area in the floor; I hit it and flipped up in the air and down I went. Pain shot through my right arm. The kids rolled toward me, but I stopped them and warned them away from the spot on the floor that had sent me flying.

I ordered them out of their skates and they helped me with mine. No one argued.

Heidi, only four, started to cry quietly, but she gathered all the snacks and put them in a little box that one of the staff handed her. Then she cuddled next to me on the floor. Although she was scared, she kept patting me. The boys stared as I sat on the floor holding my arm. The pain was incredible.

"Could I have some ice for this, please?" I called out.

"Are you broken, Mommy?" Heidi asked.

"I don't think so, honey. I think it would hurt a lot more if I were." I heard my father's chuckle at that fib because, in truth, I did fear I had broken my arm. "Here, Heidi, you carry Mommy's purse for me, okay?" She struggled into the strap of my shoulder bag while she balanced the snacks on her lap.

"There. I gots it," she said proudly.

Blake and Travis put my shoes back on for me. Some men from the roller-rink staff helped me to my feet. "Are you sure you're okay to drive?" one of them asked.

"You can do it with Brian's help," Dad's voice said in my ear. I wondered if he could be right in this case. Did he know how badly hurt I was and how close to passing out? I wished Brian had his driver's license. Luckily, he had had some practice driving, so I hoped he could help me to steer.

"Yes, I can drive," I said. I worked my way out of the rink and to the car with Brian's help. I was glad that he had come with us that day.

I fumbled in my purse left handed. "I can't get the key, Brian. You'll have to handle that. I can drive one handed, but you'd better sit beside me in case I need help turning the wheel."

The children piled into the back seat with no fuss. They were unnaturally quiet and sat eating their snacks.

"You better behave, Mom, and go to the doctor," Travis said.

"As soon as we get home, I'll get Guppy to drive me to the doctor, okay?"

I drove in silence. The pain in my arm made me woozy and I was afraid I would pass out. It took all my concentration and love for my kids to keep my head on straight. When I felt like I might lose it, I could hear my father's calm voice demanding, "Hang in there."

We made it home safely despite pain that grew steadily worse. Brian took care of the kids, and Mother drove me to the emergency room.

The doctor suspected a fracture and off I went to X-ray. There they tortured me by turning my arm at various angles that made me cry out. In between tests, I sent energy through my arm to help heal it. I had discovered that I could mend bones because I had done it for Blake a few years earlier. He had caught his bare foot between the ground and the teeter-totter of his swing set. I could see a bone pushing his skin outward as he screamed in pain. On the drive to the emergency room, I so wanted to help stop Blake's pain. No mother wants to see her child go through that. By the time the doctor looked at the X-ray of Blake's foot an hour later, all that was present was an odd, lozenge-shaped blip of light. Other indications showed that he had broken a bone—but it wasn't broken any longer.

I had no idea what I had done to heal Blake's bone, but I did it for a number of people after that. Could I do it to myself? The energy I sent through my arm relieved the pain a little, but not enough to make much difference.

Finally, the doctor returned to the exam room. He put the films of my arm on a light box and studied them closely, shaking his head. He motioned my mother over and pointed at one view.

"See that little mark there?" he asked her. Mother nodded and slid me a quick look.

"That shouldn't be there," he said.

He turned to me and continued. "I think it's a fracture, but it actually looks like a fracture that has healed." He paused and looked at me. "The nurses tell me you're some kind of psychic, and they watched you take away your son's pain and fix a broken bone in his foot when he was in here a while ago. Is that true?"

I said sheepishly, as if I had been caught at something, "It does seem that bones heal fast when I send energy through them."

I was sure that he was thinking I was crazy, but he asked, "Do you know how that works?"

"I have no idea," I told him. "I just do it."

"Did you do it today?"

I nodded.

He stared at me through narrowed eyes, then finally said, "Well it beats me. The level of pain and the bruising indicates that you landed squarely on your elbow when you fell and that you probably broke it. The fact that you remained sharp enough to drive home is amazing. I have to assume you had a fracture." He put it in a brace and sling and ordered me not to use it, warning me that there would be pain for several days. He paused and added, "At least for someone else, there would. With you, who knows?"

He wrote me a prescription and said he would send the X-rays to my orthopedist. He acted like he was afraid of me.

The rest of the day was a blur of pain, as I lay propped up on my bed. I'm allergic to many medications and couldn't take anything stronger than aspirin. Mother kept the kids busy and sent them up to peek in on me often. Their worried little faces lined up in a glum parade at my door. Blake brought me a special grub he had found, and then he got out the bug book so we could look it up. Travis worried. At last, scrubbed and tired, they hit their beds without fuss or the usual bedtime commotion.

Mom checked on me at bedtime, arranged a pile of pillows behind my back, and made sure that the phone sat next to me in easy reach. When she and I moved in together, we had agreed that we each needed our own phone line, and now that decision was coming in handy in a way I hadn't expected.

I promised I would call her if I needed anything, so she left and went downstairs to her bedroom.

I read for a long time. Then in the distance I heard strangled cries that I slowly realized were my own. I had fallen asleep and tumbled off the pillows onto my injured arm. Pain shot through me, and I reached for the phone, but it was beyond my grasp. As I pulled the cord to move the phone closer, the receiver fell off the cradle. For the second or third time, I blacked out.

My own cries brought me to a hazy state of consciousness. I thought I saw my father walk out of the shadowy corner of my room, toward my bed. Yes, it was him. He lifted me gently, hugged me, and then arranged the pillows behind me with care.

"Nance," he said, "look at the way I fixed the pillows. You won't fall with them like this."

The familiar feel and smell of him, his smile and voice—all so comforting. "I'm going downstairs to get your Mother," he told me. "You need some help." He headed out.

"I love you, Dad," I called out to him.

He turned back to me, smiling, and said, "I know you do. Believe me, I know you do." He disappeared through the closed door. He walked straight through the door, just like ghosts in the movies. It would have been funny, if my arm hadn't hurt so much.

I faded in and out of consciousness. Then Mom was beside me, her eyes wide. "Your Father woke me up. He said you needed help right away."

I nodded and told her how he had rescued me.

She said, "I was asleep, and then someone was shaking me. I thought you had come downstairs. Then I woke up enough to register who was there in the dark. He held me and whispered that he loved me. He told me to go to you. Then he disappeared."

Mom got me aspirin and we wrapped an ice pack around my elbow. She reached for my good hand and patted it absently as we sat together for awhile.

"I'm glad he comes back," I said. I had been thinking about the whole issue of the progress of his soul. "I hope we're not holding him back."

Mom said, "I wonder about that sometimes myself. But I think he's happiest near us."

"He'll never be complete without you. You are like the other half of his soul."

We sat together at 2 a.m. and wondered about our amazing situation.

Chapter 19

The Storm

I had made an appointment for Heidi with a specialist in Philadelphia because she had a speech impediment that made it difficult for her to communicate verbally and was delaying her speech development. She was a rather uncooperative five year old, so I had promised her that after the appointment we would drive over to Bryn Mawr to visit my boyfriend, Steve.

I had first met Steve when he came to interview me for an article. I had opened the door to see a nice-looking, blonde young man, and I instantly sensed that I would marry him. Such an idea startled me, and I ushered him into my office with my scrapbooks and told him I'd be back shortly. I went into my living room to try to calm down. I was so sure that, with my unusual job, I would never even be asked out on a date again let alone become involved with someone. After the painful ending of my first marriage, I wasn't looking for a relationship; I needed time to heal and get on my feet.

In the living room I meditated briefly and then went back into my office to do the interview with this young man. I did my best to block out the "knowing"—a certainty of something that comes through psychically— that I had just experienced. It was a strange way to start a relationship, but we did indeed begin to date and in a unique way we clicked. Steve lived in a Philadelphia suburb, and he invited Heidi and me to meet him at his apartment after the doctor's appointment and then drive to Parkesburg, Pennsylvania, to visit with his family. Heidi liked Steve and the idea of seeing him afterward helped her to behave while we were at the appointment.

The sky looked threatening when we got to Steve's apartment. The weather reports predicted periodic light showers, which didn't sound too bad. We got ready to leave for the drive to Parkesburg, and Heidi decided she wanted to ride with Steve. She liked his little car, a white Mazda, and she particularly liked his attention.

In fact, that first day Steve came to do the interview, Heidi, just arrived home from school, looked Steve up and down, pushed her little glasses up on her nose, and said, "You're going to be my next daddy." I was mortified. Steve blanched but leaned down to talk to her kindly. I wanted to wring her neck, but I understood that things just pop out of a psychic child unbidden. Part of me worried about Heidi and how having this skill would make her life difficult. At the moment, she was busy charming Steve as only Heidi could.

Steve and I were both a little worried about Heidi riding as his passenger because she didn't know him very well. What if she changed her mind mid-trip? We assured her that I would be following them because I didn't know where Parkesburg was. As we traveled, I could see her little hand waving at me every now and then. I waved back and on we went.

It was rush hour and all three lanes of the expressway were full. We had merged from a left-hand ramp and ended up in the fast lane. I saw Steve put his turn signal on, but no one allowed us to move over a lane, so there we were, stuck. I didn't mind as long as I could see where he was.

I noticed the traffic ahead slowing down fast into a sea of brake lights. Before I could figure out what was going on, a wall of rain hit our cars, the kind of deluge that hits areas close to the coast. The rain came down so hard it blinded me. I slowed to a crawl, turned up the wipers, and snapped on my emergency blinkers. I hoped that would make me more visible.

I felt my left tires hit rough pavement and realized I was going off the road. Easing the wheel to the right, I could feel the tug of heavy water pushing against my wheels.

I decided to use my psychic ability to keep me safe because I couldn't see a thing. I had read about psychics driving blindfolded and managing not to hit anything. I hoped it would work for me as it felt like I was floating in a void. I had no idea if there were cars in front or beside me. All I could see was a torrent of rain.

I was wondering if it might be safer if I pulled onto the median when I heard my father say in a forceful voice, "No! The median is full of cars spread all over the place. Stay where you are, and I will tell you where you can move safely."

I drove hunched over the steering wheel trying to see what was around me but I was still driving blind. I could feel the water on the road getting deeper, but I was afraid to slow down because I might be rear-ended. Usually, driving rains like this went as fast as they came, but not this one. The minutes dragged by and on I went.

I tried not to think about Heidi. Steve did not have my psychic skills, and I wondered how on earth he could keep her safe. I used the edge of the road as a guide to keep going in the general direction I was headed when the storm hit. The scary part for me was that I had no idea where Steve's parents lived. With no mental picture of the roads, I was pretty much stranded.

"There's room in the lane to your right," Dad said in a much calmer voice. "Move into it slowly, and I'll tell you when to straighten the wheel."

I edged over slowly, expecting a crash at any minute.

"Straighten the wheel now." I did as I was told, and drove on through the torrent. Finally he said, "There's room to your right again and an off-ramp." It was the same patient tone he always used with me when he was teaching me how to do something. "Start pulling to the right now. That's my girl! Now, keep on moving slowly to the right. You'll feel that you're coming up a slight elevation. You're at the end of the ramp and you need to stop now." I felt him pat my shoulder.

I thought I saw a glow of lights ahead of me, as if some big buildings were there. Suddenly, the curtain of rain parted just enough so that I could see a little better at last.

"There's a shopping mall," he said. "Drive into that parking lot and look for the public phones inside the mall. That's where you'll find Steve." I had no idea why I would find Steve inside some strange mall. What were the chances that we would land in the same place after driving blind in that awful storm for almost an hour? Even though I did not understand Dad's statement that Steve would be there, I prayed he was right. I was terrified that he and Heidi were back there somewhere in a crash or off the road, stranded.

As I searched for a parking spot, I asked, "Are they all right? Is Heidi scared?"

Dad answered, "They're safe. Steve was careful and he's familiar with the roads. Heidi kept giving him pep talks and, of course, she's so little she didn't realize how dangerous it was. And as you know, she has some of your abilities."

I wound my way around the parking area in the mall until I could find a spot to park. The lots were full, as others had sought refuge from the storm. I locked my car and ran through the rain to the mall entrance. I asked the first person I saw when I got in the mall where the phones were located and hurried in the direction she pointed. My plan was to call Steve's family and find out if they had heard from him and use the opportunity to get directions to their house from wherever I was. As I ran, I tried in vain to see some indication of the name of the mall.

Thank God there were intact phone books with the bank of phones. Steve's family's name is spelled uniquely, and I had no trouble finding them. Steve's dad answered right away, and he tried to help me figure out where I was, and asked where Steve was. I told him about the storm and had to admit that I did not know if he was all right. "Heidi is with him, and I am worried sick about both of them," I stammered.

Suddenly, I heard a wonderfully familiar little voice: "See, I told you Mommy wasn't lost," Heidi said to Steve. "There she is. You got lost but Mommy didn't."

She ran into my arms and I stood dumbfounded staring at them. Dad was right. They were in the same place that I was.

I could tell from Heidi's ongoing narrative that she was not scared at all. I mouthed, "Thank you," to Steve as I realized his dad was yelling into the phone to get me to tell him what was going on. I handed the phone to a surprised Steve so he could assure his father that he was fine.

We were a little too shaken to drive anywhere, and we didn't know if the storm still raged. We walked to the food court and grabbed a bite to eat. I could not stop shivering from the stress of that long drive in the torrent.

Steve said, "How on earth did you find this mall? You don't know the area!"

"Let's just say I had a little help," I said with a sigh of relief. "I was driving blind, and then my dad started helping me. I can't believe that neither one of us was in an accident!"

Steve nodded at Heidi; he and I had been dating long enough by now that he was aware of my father's occasional help. As a reporter, he was a professional skeptic, which was a strain on me, but he had learned that there was something going on with me that defied logic. I don't think he was happy about it, because he wanted a simple explanation for these phenomena, and he didn't like the fact that he couldn't find one. Most of the time he clung to his skepticism, but this experience was raising some doubts.

He told me, "I had a little helper who kept announcing when there were no cars beside me so that I could get off the road. I just figured she had your abilities, so I listened to her. We've been at the mall for a while looking for you. Heidi insisted that you were here. I finally decided to call my parents to see if you called them and try to figure out where to go, and there you were, already on the phone talking to my dad! I have to say that this is way beyond coincidence."

I laughed, "Are we actually convincing a skeptic?"

He said, "You don't know this area and you couldn't have had any idea where we were going. Neither one of us could see a darn thing, yet we ended up at the same mall. Either it's a massive coincidence or you're both psychic. There are a bunch of other roads you could have turned onto, yet you ended up here and so did we. It's remarkable."

Heidi looked up from her pizza. "Now, I did tell you, Steve, that Mommy wasn't lost. You were lost." She grinned in saucy satisfaction.

After we ate, we still needed to get to his parents' house. There was no time to talk as the storm had delayed us quite a bit, and I still had to drive back to Newark and get Heidi to bed to be ready for school the next day. I took Heidi's hand out of habit as we walked through the mall toward my car. Suddenly, Heidi yanked on my arm so hard that it knocked me off balance. In a stage whisper that Steve could plainly hear she announced, "Mommy, I got to go with Steve. He gets lost, you know."

I looked at Steve; he shrugged as Heidi walked over and took charge of his arm. Outside, the rain was gone and the sun blazed. What a strange day. Then I saw my car and in the next row was Steve's Mazda, parked facing my car. Could this get any stranger?

My visit with Steve's parents was brief out of necessity. I now had a sleepy child who grew grouchier by the minute. I drove south to Delaware while Heidi fell asleep in the back seat. I occupied my mind wondering how Dad had pulled off the trick of reuniting me with Steve and Heidi. Obviously, he knew what was going on in their car up ahead of me. Dad must have pulled his two-places-at-the-same-time routine again, like he had done years ago when he visited Susan and me at the same moment 1,200 miles apart, with Susan near Chicago and me in Newark. This was a part of his existence that was even harder to comprehend than his appearances.

As a child growing up in South America I had heard a story about how Jesus had walked that continent at the same time He was in the Middle East, halfway across the world. I used to wonder about that, but now I understood. He was in the Light of Life, so by simply thinking about the places, He could be in both at once.

Now, through Dad, I learned that some things are simply miraculous and unknowable but nevertheless quite real. I was fortunate that I didn't fall into the negative habits that many of us do—denying a reality unfolding in front of us simply because it doesn't make sense with what we know and understand of the world. I took the approach that I know this just happened, and I can't explain it logically, but I know it *did* happen.

I have concluded over the years that human knowledge of physics is too limited, and our present understanding of space and time is either incorrect or incomplete. I have had the good fortune to discuss this with a few physicists, and they agree with me and are interested to hear of my experiences that challenge accepted concepts. I have left them curious, as I have been, to theorize how these things might have happened rather than merely sit there in denial. I moved from one incredible experience to the next with an open mind and great fascination as I learned more about the amazing things the human mind is capable of.

"Thanks, Dad, for keeping us safe," I said to the air as I drove. I heard him happily whistling Zip-a-dee-doo-dah in response.

On the 11 o'clock news I watched TV coverage of the storm hitting that long stretch of road. The newscaster said it had been some freak weather pattern with high winds and possibly a microburst. The footage, taken after it started to clear up by a TV truck that had been caught in the deluge, showed that vehicles had pulled off the roads at random. Dad was right to tell me not to pull onto the median. The news video revealed piles of damaged cars—like Blake's room when he pulled out all his toys. I watched in horror as the footage showed crash after crash, cars in tangles with responders trying to help the injured. I was mesmerized by the destruction we had passed through without a scratch—Dad and I in one car, Steve and Heidi in the other.

The news coverage shifted to footage taken from a helicopter and showing a tangled mess along the highway. I recognized the mall we had both driven to. The ramp I drove up was blocked by cars except for a narrow channel that was shown on TV. It was now full of rescue vehicles. That must have been the path Dad took me through. Seeing the aerial footage made me realize how amazing it was—even more than I had realized—that Steve, Heidi, and I had arrived at the same safe spot at the same moment.

Chapter 20

Attempted Murder

In the early 1980s, I had been divorced for a while and had moved to western Pennsylvania, leaving my mother back in Delaware alone. That was one of the hardest things I had ever had to do. After the divorce, Mother and I had agreed that this might be the safest scenario for me and for my children, but it broke our hearts to be that far apart. A young woman from Pittsburgh I had met offered to help me move to the area and to introduce me to people there, so that I could restart my business a safe distance from some hard things that had happened in Delaware due to my work—a consequence of helping the police to apprehend criminals. I wanted a new start for my family.

I had been granted full custody, and the custody agreement allowed me to move to another area as long as I permitted my ex-husband visitation rights. Unfortunately, I got sick just after I moved to Pennsylvania and could not drive the four to five hours it took to take the children back to Delaware for a visit. The Delaware courts were still handling some of the issues from the divorce that had not been settled, and the judge, a woman, angered by my move and skeptical about my unusual job, referred to me in court as a "gypsy" and speculated where I might set up my tent next. She took custody away from me because of that one missed visit. Now my ex-husband had custody, and my life became a nightmare. Every other weekend I drove the four or five hours each way from Greensburg,

Pennsylvania, to Newark, Delaware, to visit with my children.

One weekend my sons were quite upset. They cried a lot, which wasn't typical of them. They kept talking about my getting hurt driving home. I didn't know what to think about their strange behavior. Normally, I would have started the long drive home right after taking the children back to their father's, but this time I felt reluctant to leave. Instead, I went back to my mother's house and we talked about the situation.

Finally, I knew I had to get on the road, as clients had scheduled time with me the next morning. When I left, both Mother and I were edgy in ways we usually were not. I didn't know if it was the boys' comments or my own inner warnings that were making me uneasy. As I drove, I was immersed in thoughts about the projects I had scheduled for the coming week. I had always loved to drive, and I would plan out my week while I made the long trek.

Darkness had fallen by the time I reached the area around Avondale, Pennsylvania, a part of the state not far from my mother's home in Newark. I liked this back-roads route to the Pennsylvania Turnpike. The countryside was lovely, and going this way shaved a substantial amount of time off the long drive to Greensburg. Traffic had been sparse until now, but all of a sudden I was stuck in a slow-moving line of cars headed into a small town near Avondale. This town was on my regular route up to the turnpike, and I always loved the eerie glow of its daylight street lamps, which made the town look like an old movie set. My attention fastened on a blue pickup truck that was sitting on a side street well ahead of me on the left. The shape of the vehicle reminded me of my grandfather's beat-up old Ford pickup. I couldn't take my eyes off it.

The closer I came to the truck, the more concerned I felt. In my head I heard my father's calm voice, "Do exactly what I tell you to do when I tell you to do it." His tone was grave, and I took it as a direct warning that some kind of crash was about to happen. The pickup pulled out of the side street and approached on the opposite side of the road; traffic was moving slowly, so I could keep track of the truck as well as the cars that were in front of me.

The truck got closer and closer, and my father's voice said, "Slam on the brakes hard when I tell you to." I could tell there were two people in the truck, and I could feel danger emanating from every inch of it. The truck kept veering toward me.

As the truck's cab approached the nose of my car, I could see that a man was driving with one hand and holding what looked like a pistol with the other. The hair stood up on my neck.

In slow motion I saw him aim the gun right at my head! Dad yelled, "Brake hard now!" I slammed on the brakes just as the driver fired at my head. In shock, I watched the muzzle flash and saw a streak of red go across in front of my windshield. I looked away from the streak right into the face of the man who had fired at me. His face showed shock as I looked right at him.

My father's calm voice jolted me alert. "Foot off the brake and move ahead." As I did that, the driver of the pickup floored the gas pedal and the truck took off. I tried to read the license plate, but the lights around it were out and darkness obscured the plate's numbers and letters. All I knew was that the truck was blue, an old pickup, and it seemed to have a Delaware license plate.

I had no doubt that the man had just tried to kill me. He hadn't tried to kill just anyone; he was waiting for *me*. When I was sure he was no longer in sight, I pulled to the side of the road. I was shaking uncontrollably. I tried to recapture what I had seen and memorize the details of it. An unexpected knock on my car window produced another jolt. Was he back to try again?

I looked up to see a stranger, a man, who said, "Are you okay?" I looked in the rear view mirror and recognized the car that had been immediately behind mine.

I opened the window. "I'm shaken up, but okay. Did you see what happened?"

"That crazy fool nearly hit you!" said the man. "He pulled right alongside and I thought he was going to crash into you. And then he shot at you! What is going on with this world?"

I took a breath and said, "I'm going to the State Police barracks and report this."

"That was crazy," he said. "Are you sure you're okay?"

"Yeah, I'm just scared," I said, trying to will myself to stop shaking.

The stranger said, "I'll call the police from my house and tell them what I saw. I hope they catch him."

I asked if he had gotten the license plate; he hadn't, but I thanked him for checking on me.

The man said, "I wasn't going to leave you here to bleed to death! I wanted to see if he shot you. I just can't believe what I saw. I'm so glad you're all right."

The shock was wearing off, and I realized that my champion and I were sitting ducks if we stayed on the same stretch of road. I turned my car around and drove to the barracks to report the incident. The trooper was concerned; maybe to lighten the mood he told me that it was April Fool's Day and all kinds of crazy things were happening. I knew my description didn't give him much to go on, but I was certain the attack wasn't random. The officer got me a cup of hot chocolate and made sure I was calmed down enough to drive safely.

Back in the car I faced driving through the same stretch of road again. Dad's voice assured me, "It won't happen again. The fact that you stopped just as he shot scared him. He knows what you do for a living, and he's terrified now." More confirmation that I wasn't some random victim. I spent the rest of the long drive back to Greensburg trying to figure out how my sons had known this danger was coming for me and who would want me dead.

The next morning I called some good friends in law enforcement and described to them what had happened. Their questions made me realize that the dashboard lights were out inside the truck as well as the license plate lights outside. Their conclusion: it was a professional hit and I was lucky to be alive. That was terrifying. Someone had paid to have me killed!

In the days that followed I stretched my abilities to pick up some sense of who targeted me for death. I had no proof, but I came to the conclusion that it was revenge for a case in which I had helped the police put away a killer. Did I have to fear being the target of every criminal I helped the police bring to justice? Could I go on with my work in the face of that threat?

I started to feel relieved when my friends on the police force put the word out that I was an undercover cop and that anyone hurting me would have the full attention of law enforcement. But the greatest assurance of my future safety came from my father. I heard him say, "The person who tried to shoot you won't come near you and is spreading it all over that you are a witch. He realized you knew he was going to shoot you. He is afraid of you."

Looking that killer right in the eyes was a terrifying moment. I have my father's ghost, my sons' warnings, and my psychic abilities to thank for the fact that I am still alive.

Chapter 21
The Pearls

Once in a while I start work on a missing person's case expecting the usual result—that the person is deceased—only to end up pleasantly surprised. This is what happened with baby Billy. Members of the baby's family brought the case to me in the form of a map marked with the location where Billy's mother was standing when the child was yanked from her arms by her soon-to-be-ex husband.

They had just split up, and the father was trying to take advantage of the fact that the custody hearing was scheduled, but no custody agreement was yet in place. The mother had to race to obtain an emergency order of custody just so law enforcement could assist in looking for the child. The judge granted her full custody, and notification was sent to the father's address and to his family members that Billy's disappearance was now listed as a kidnapping and they should immediately notify the police of the whereabouts of father and baby. Neither the father nor his family responded to this order.

The family members who came to me for help had only a formal portrait of the baby and several snapshots. Billy was nine months old.

I started trying to range the child and realized I had a problem. Often when I'm ranging, I can actually see through the subject's eyes. But Billy was so young and so small that I couldn't get a fix on his position by what he was able to see. He was busy looking at his toes, his fingers, and sometimes a toy. I had never tried to find a baby this young before. I had no idea what to do.

"Range the adult, not the child," suggested the voice of Dad in my head. "You can jump from the baby's mind to that of the adult who's with him."

I tried it and it worked rather well. From the vantage point of the adult sitting inside a big truck, an 18-wheeler, I recognized the signs marking the border between Pennsylvania and Ohio on the Pennsylvania Turnpike. I could feel Billy's father thinking about going to his uncle's house in Ohio. I saw route numbers and some landmarks.

Armed with all the detail I could provide, the family left to share the information with the police. Shortly thereafter I got a call from law enforcement officers working the case. They had checked the uncle's house, and the father had stopped there but was gone by the time that authorities arrived. Did I know where he was now? I found that I could not get any new images that would help to pinpoint the location of Billy and his father. Rather than ranging their current location, I tried to use my precognitive abilities to predict where they would be the next day. The police were checking on all the information I was providing; it was accurate, but it was a day behind. I began to work harder to get ahead of Billy's father.

The next time I ranged I felt that the father was headed back into Pennsylvania, the baby still with him. Then I got an image of a grocery store that I recognized from a previous case, and I called my police contact right away and relayed the latest information.

"There's a grocery store in Pennsylvania. You need to go there right away," I said, and I pinpointed its location. "There's a woman in that store right now and the baby is with her. She is related to the kidnapper and taking care of the baby for him—if you can just get there fast enough."

The officers hung up the phone and I waited impatiently to find out what happened. Two hours later I got a call from Billy's grandmother.

"They got him back and he's fine!" she exclaimed. "He's been well taken care of; he was with his father's sister. They've both been arrested. Thank you so much for finding Billy." I was as relieved as she was that the baby had been found.

After all the terrible times I had worked cases that ended up with bodies, this was a gift. It felt so good to help to return a child, alive and well, to his family. Forever after when things got bad, I would savor the memory of the day we found Billy.

By now I had been living in Greensburg, Pennsylvania, for some time. Steve and I had married in 1982, fulfilling what I had known and Heidi had predicted.

A woman came to me in tears to report that her 16-year-old daughter, Ashley, was missing. She brought photos and a map showing where the girl was last seen. The mother checked with all the girl's friends, and it seemed that no one had any idea where the young lady was now.

As soon as I looked at the photo showing Ashley and began to range, I got excited. "She's alive!" I blurted out. "She's with a young man she thinks she's in love with, and they're going south. They're headed for Georgia, where he has family."

I gave Ashley's mother a description of the young man, and I expressed concern because he was in his 20s and the girl was only 16.

My client had no idea who the man might be, but she took the information to the police. Unbeknownst to her mom, Ashley had been dating this young man for almost three months. The police got that information from one of her girlfriends.

Now that they knew the name of the missing girl's companion, the authorities started combing through his relatives and discovered he had a cousin living in Georgia. The search began, and I worked with law enforcement to help them locate these young people. Through my ranging I could tell the police about the areas the couple was traveling through en route to Georgia.

I also worked with Ashley's mother to prepare her for the fact that when the young lady returned from her journey, she was going to need counseling for quite some time. I advised this woman that, as a mother, she must refrain from anger because she would have to work hard to help her daughter get over the mistake she had made.

One of the man's relatives admitted to police that he had tipped off the guy that the cops were after him. I could sense that they had changed directions and let the authorities and Ashley's mother know that they were now headed back toward Pennsylvania. They were picked up by the police on their way back. By that point Ashley was being held against her will by her supposed boyfriend, who had raped and beaten her. She tried to get away, and he handcuffed and chained her to prevent escape. She was now badly frightened and truly happy to be rescued by the police.

Once she was back at home, her mother had the wisdom to bring Ashley to meet me, and I tried to help this young lady not to be so hard on herself for falling for this man. I advised her that it would take her a long time to get over her mistake, but, as I had also foreseen and told her mother, the girl did recover, went to college, and is now happily raising her own family.

In my line of work, cases like Billy and Ashley are like pearls on a wonderful necklace. I run my fingers over those pearls in my mind, and they bring me comfort when other cases end up badly. They also give me faith in humanity when the authorities are willing to try anything to help find a missing child. Law enforcement officers take a lot of heat, but the men and women I have had the honor to work with have stretched themselves all over the world trying to solve cases that have driven them mad with frustration. Every once in a while in the course of these investigations, we gather another pearl.

And sometimes the pearl takes another form: removing a killer from the streets.

141

Chapter 22

A Psychic Family

As Heidi grew, she would occasionally repeat telekinetic acts like she had shown us with her ball when she was just a baby. Her most startling feat happened when the boys and I took her to a bowling alley for the first time. At six, she couldn't lift the ball herself, so we helped her carry it to the edge of the lane. She gave the ball a shove, and it wobbled down the alley and right into the gutter. "That doesn't count!" said Heidi. "I get another turn, right?" We all agreed that was fair since it was her first time bowling.

Her second try was just as bad, but as the ball started to roll into the gutter, it stopped, teetered on the edge of the gutter, and slowly and deliberately rolled back up to her waiting hands. "I got it, go again!" she squealed. We were all laughing so hard, none of us moved fast enough to take the ball away from her.

She shoved the ball back down the lane, and when it started to head for the gutter, she stomped her foot, pointed at the recalcitrant ball, and somehow mentally pushed it where she wanted it to go. Weaving back and forth across the lane, the ball made its slow progress toward the pins, and knocked down half of them.

"I got a score, I got a score!" she exclaimed.

Travis explained, "You get another turn now because you hit some pins, Heidi."

He did not have to make the offer twice. We lifted the ball for her and placed it at the top of the lane. She gave it a mighty shove and then in her imperious manner, aimed the ball down the lane. Much less wobble this time, as it headed right for the middle of the pins. It crashed into them, and all but one toppled. Absolutely furious that all the pins didn't come down, she pointed at the one pin still teetering and knocked it over. A cheer went up behind us, and I turned to see a small crowd watching.

A man at the next lane with too much beer in him was having some trouble with Heidi's abilities. "Weird kid, weird kid, weird kid," he kept muttering to himself.

We bowled our way back around to Heidi's turn. Travis explained to her where she needed to hit the pins in order to get a strike. We watched her aim the ball down its wobbly path until it bashed into the pins just to the left of where it needed to be. She brought down all but two pins.

On her next try she got a strike. Everyone cheered; everyone but the man in the next lane. "I'm never drinking again," he exclaimed. "I must have the DTs. Nobody can do what that kid did." He packed up his stuff and stomped out. Everyone clapped as he left.

"Can we go home now, Mommy?" said Heidi. "This is too much hard work and my head hurts."

As Heidi grew, her temper also developed, and interesting things happened when she got angry. It was not unusual for light bulbs to blow out when she was really angry, and sometimes objects slid across the table on their own. One day when she was about nine, she got so angry at her brothers that she imploded her favorite wastebasket, which was made of metal. She burst into tears and said, "Mom, how do I stop this?"

I told her I could help her learn to release energy from her mind before it did damage. "Picture your anger as a basketball and throw it away into something big and sturdy, like an imaginary dumpster."

For a while, images like that helped. I spent less money on replacement light bulbs, and our wastebaskets remained uncrumpled. But when she reached puberty things got crazy.

Heidi and I had worked together to come up with outlets for her energy that caused less destruction in her environment. I taught her how to use all that power to heal people, and this worked as a release valve. But there wasn't enough of that kind of work available to her in a private way to exhaust all her energy.

"Buy some thick silverware and show her how to bend it with her mind," my dad suggested. His sudden appearance was a surprise; he hadn't been around for several months.

"If I teach her to bend silverware," I said, "I won't have a straight piece of cutlery in the house!"

He said, "She needs an outlet for that energy; otherwise, it's going to damage her health. Try it out. You'll have fewer exploding light bulbs and a happier daughter." At this, he disappeared.

The next day I went to a resale shop and bought some sturdy flatware for Heidi to practice with. I wasn't sure it would work, but she took to it quickly. In a matter of seconds she bent every tine on the first fork. She tried a spoon with the same result.

It occurred to me that we shouldn't be doing this exercise in the kitchen near my silverware drawer. I pulled the drawer open. "I think we better practice somewhere else because you're bending the tines on the silver in the drawer." We both laughed but it wasn't exactly funny. Where could she practice where there wasn't metal around that she might affect?

After a few days, Heidi announced that she had been practicing with the flatware in her room. She sat on her bed and placed a fork on her desk across the room. As she bent spoons and knives on the bed, she concentrated on not harming the fork on the desk. "At first they all bent," she explained, "but I figured out how to do it so I didn't mess up the one on my desk. And you know what else? I haven't had as many headaches, and I'm not getting angry as easily."

"Mom, get her some more silverware," wisecracked 14-year-old, six-foot-tall Travis, who was eating at the kitchen table.

Heidi and I both laughed.

As the children grew, each of them developed their own way of using their particular psychic abilities. Travis continued to have precognitive experiences, and Blake's skill at finding things sharpened as he grew. I was glad that Blake had that skill as he constantly forgot where he put things. Travis also developed the ability to read people. His information was quite exact and far greater than the average person's instincts. He would know quickly what kind of person he was looking at—not exactly in the way that I did, but he could size people up very accurately. I knew his skill would come in handy once he was in the working world—that is, if he had not outgrown it, as often happens.

It wasn't until Travis was 15 that I realized he also had other talents. We were on a trip and stopped at a restaurant to have dinner. Travis kept staring around the dining area as if something had spooked him.

"Are you all right Travis?" I asked.

"I had a dream last night," he told me, "and I saw this place in my dream. I mean, even the same people sitting at the same tables! Is that weird or what?"

"Not if you have precognitive abilities," I answered.

"Mom's three-dollar words!" he grumbled with the kind of distaste that only a teenager can muster.

"Sorry about that," I said. "Precognitive means having the ability to see things that are going to happen in the future. Some people can actually do that when they're awake, and others do it when they're asleep."

He thought about it. "That's kind of neat. Is that how you do your work?"

"Sometimes, but I also have other abilities."

"So I'm kind of like you?" Travis asked.

"Yes, you certainly are."

I often wondered how three genetically different children ended up in the same family with a mother who understood and lived with psychic abilities. To my mind, it was no coincidence. Although many children have minor psychic skills, few display the strong abilities that Blake, Travis, and Heidi did. It was easy to understand how Heidi could inherit psychic abilities, but in the cases of Blake and Travis, perhaps the path was somehow planned for them or we were drawn to one another. Somehow, we had come together as a psychic family.

My kids were growing up, and my father didn't visit as often now. It seemed natural for him to move on with his own progress, just as I was getting on with my life. And I was okay with that. I didn't want to tie Dad's spirit to our lives simply because I missed him. I guessed that it was natural to feel this way and that most grieving people adjust eventually and think of their loved ones less and less often. I really had no frame of reference for how non-psychic people experience the death of a loved one. I had never heard anyone else talk about communicating with dead relatives so I figured they don't. I hid the fact that I was talking to my father's ghost from pretty much everyone but my immediate family. On the few occasions that I alluded to it, people thought I was nuts. So, I took it as normal for me but probably not for others. No matter how much time passed between Dad's visits, however, he was always there whenever my family was in crisis.

Chapter 23
Mother's Progress

Before I left Delaware for Pennsylvania, Mother started dating a man named Felix. He was a retired chemist for a prominent corporation located in Delaware. Their romance bloomed, and she eloped for the second time in her life.

I teased her, "Didn't you want a wedding with family and all?"

"Felix and I thought about it but just didn't want the fuss at our age."

"Well, congratulations," I told her. "I'm so happy for you," What I didn't tell her was that I felt apprehension. This was not a man who loved Mother the way my father had. Felix had asked me a lot of questions about Mother's finances when he first met her. I knew the stories about older widows getting ripped off by men they married later in life. In fact, I had worked cases like that for families trying to regain money stolen by such husbands. I was concerned; I had been around law enforcement long enough to acquire that professional police "paranoia"—a suspicious attitude toward everyone that develops from working so many criminal cases. I did my best, however, to meet our new family member half way.

Mother and Felix took some lovely trips together out west. They went whitewater rafting—to the shock of her grandchildren, who could not imagine their Guppy being a risk taker like that. After they went up in a hot air balloon that crashed, Travis got upset and said, "Mom, don't you think you should tell them to stop doing these crazy things?"

"Your grandmother is an adult," I responded, "and she's my mom. I can't tell her what to do, but I will tell her you're worried about her."

My second son's glare let me know that this was not a satisfactory answer. The two younger children had been returned to my custody by now, and I called Mother often to give her reports of their progress. She missed them terribly. On my next call to her Delaware home, I told her, "Travis is worried. He thinks you and Felix are doing too many dangerous things."

She chuckled. "You tell him thank you for me." She hesitated. "But maybe don't tell him that our next trip is to Alaska and we're going heli-hopping!" I had no idea what that was. She said, "A helicopter flies you up onto a glacier and drops you off. You have lunch on the glacier and get to explore it. Isn't that neat?" Her excitement pulsed through the phone.

I was beginning to think that Travis's concerns might be based in reality. I said, "It certainly is an adventure." My mom and stepdad were taking some interesting but risky trips. My psychic abilities told me she would be fine, but the logical half of me was growing anxious. I often struggled to balance my two halves, especially when the safety of people I loved was at stake.

Mom said, "The tour company assures us that it's sunny and warm on the glacier, but just for Travis I'll pack heavier clothes anyway. Tell him not to worry. I'll be careful."

Mother and Dad had always wanted to explore the United States, but hadn't had much opportunity. All our travel overseas had not dampened Mom's appetite for adventure. I remembered a trip down the mountains to the coast of Ecuador when I was about 15. I recalled the trouble Dad had negotiating hairpin curves and deep-rutted dirt roads in our low-slung American station wagon.

At one point on that trip, the car broke down, and Dad got out his ever-present tools and coveralls. Mother herded us over to the inside shoulder of the road, away from the straight drop down the side of the mountain. She spread a blanket on the ground and laid out a picnic lunch. "Come on, Fred. You might as well eat something before you tackle the car. It's probably going to take a while."

"Yep, afraid so," he said as he slid out from under the car. "Have to get out the cotton and raisins again." This was a mixture he used to plug any hole that the rough roads caused. It was easy to mix and hardened quickly. He wiped his hands on his handkerchief and plopped down beside us to the sight of a perfect, ready-to-eat meal. "That's my city girl, always ready for anything." He leaned over and ruffled her hair.

As we ate, Mom said, "Look at that view."

I looked down at the jagged mountainside covered with lush vegetation. Banana trees and jungle were everywhere. It looked like green velvet covering the rugged crevasses. I thought I could see a hint of blue water way in the distance. "Is that the ocean over there?" I asked.

"That it is, sharp eyes." Dad smiled at me. His sandwich had disappeared in an instant as usual. He climbed to his feet and said, "I have to get this car fixed before dusk. We don't know what the animal population up here is."

He started to work as Mother busied us with plans to explore carefully around the road. She reminded us which spiders and snakes to watch out for as she pulled out her watercolor supplies and little milk jug with water in it. She was going to paint the view.

The part of the road I wanted to explore involved a climb. I had been ascending for a while when I felt that I was being watched. Nervous that it might be a puma or some other wild animal, I turned around ever so slowly. Munching away right next to me was a large goat. I checked out the fact that he had thick horns and a beard. I froze. The annoyed goat snorted his displeasure at my intrusion onto his territory and then stopped chewing. That was not good. "Dad!" I hollered. "I need you now!"

Far down at the road, my father inched out from under the car. Still on his back he looked up to survey what I had gotten into. "Do not move!" he called out to me.

He jumped to his feet and hurried toward me. I remained still. The urgent tone in Dad's voice let me know there was something odd about that goat. I had no choice but to continue to watch him, although I avoided looking him straight in the eye in case that would make him madder. Too late. He started to back up. He pawed the earth and glared at me with his horns lowered.

"Dad, I think he's going to charge!" I wailed.

The sound of my voice brought the goat's head up for a moment. He had long white fur and looked much larger and more filled out than the domestic goats I was used to. Down went the goat's head again just as Dad arrived, breathing hard from the climb. He was below me on the hill and now I was between the goat and my father. He had his pistol with him.

Dad said, "This is a mountain goat. I want you to climb away from him and slide down behind me."

His voice was calm but impelling. He sounded that way only when I was in danger. The goat turned his attention to the bigger target my father made, as I edged my way down until I was right behind him. The animal pawed and snorted and made a short charge, but then pulled up. Dad calmly raised his pistol and aimed.

I started to cry. "Please don't shoot him, Daddy! He was just having his lunch. I scared him."

"I can see that," he said calmly. "I won't shoot unless he charges."

Dad started to back away down the mountain as I descended below him. The goat made another short charge that brought him really close to my dad. I slid down as fast as I could. To heck with getting dirty—I was leaving that goat alone! Down below, Mother stood in front of Susan and me as Dad backed slowly down the mountain. The goat followed too closely and snorted and made short charges.

"Harriet," Dad barked, "take the kids farther down the road."

Mother shooed us away from the confrontation. Susan and I were crying. Mother stood in front of us ready to defend us, but all she had for a weapon was her milk can. She held the lid in one hand and the bottom in the other. I guess she thought that clanging it might scare the goat away, but I didn't think that the determined goat was going to be dissuaded by a little noise.

Once my father reached a certain level close to the car, the goat stopped. Dad spoke soothingly to him as he always did with frightened animals, and the goat stopped pawing the ground. That was good. He just stood there watching us. Finally, he put his head down and started grazing. Somehow he had decided we were no longer a threat. He grazed and watched us as he chewed contentedly.

"It's okay, Harriet," Dad called. He holstered his gun as he walked over to us. "He's reached the edge of what he considers his territory. As long as we don't challenge his space, we should be fine." He gave Mom a hug and said, "That's my girl." All the while he kept a weather eye on the goat.

Then, my father looked at me and shook his head. "Of course, you had to go and find a mountain goat, and then you had to cross into his territory." He smiled down at me as I hung my head. It was another near disaster because I wasn't watching where I was going.

He went on, "You're lucky it wasn't a puma; he wouldn't have backed off. Now stay close to the road while I finish up!"

Mother moved the blanket and her sketch materials farther away from the mountain goat, and she and I settled down on the blanket for an uneasy wait. Susan hung around Dad, keeping a close eye on the goat.

I asked, "Mom, how come you and Dad get along so well and other kids' parents don't?" I had been saving that question for a long time.

She looked at me and smiled. "Your father and I felt complete together from the moment we met. When we looked at each other, I felt at peace. I don't know exactly how to explain that to you, but it was like I had always known him. And even when he's aggravating me to pieces, he still gives me that sense of peace."

"How can he aggravate you like that *and* give you peace?"

"He just does. I don't know why but it's wonderful, and I wish more people had it."

I considered her answer. "You're lucky, Mom."

"Yes I am," she beamed, "and so are you. Look who you have for a daddy."

We both watched Dad working under the car waiting for him to wriggle out and announce, "Well, are you guys ready to go? Because I am!"

Chapter 24
A Warning

One day after Mom and Felix had been together for seven years, I finished my last appointment before the kids got home from school. I sat in my home office in Greensburg and watched the squirrels chase each other around the yard. My backyard was like a small forest, and three young squirrels played there all the time, putting on hilarious shows for us. I was tired and having a few moments of silence was a welcome respite. I sat there and drank it in. Suddenly, Dad was there, sitting awkwardly on the couch across from me.

"This couch feels like it could swallow me," he quipped. "But it's comfortable." It was the kind of moment we had shared a thousand times when he was alive. He got right to the point: "I'm concerned about your mother. You know things are not going well with her husband, don't you?"

After a few years of traveling, she and Felix had gotten their adventures out of their systems. Both were aging, and although they seemed in fairly good health, she had confided she was tired of doing all the housework and cooking with no help. Plus, she didn't like being stuck in Delaware so far away from her grandchildren and me, so she was researching retirement communities in my area. Felix was frightened to move and becoming quite difficult to deal with. He would often get upset and yell at Mother, and this was not something she had ever experienced with my father. I knew that Dad would be more aware than I of what was going on—given his vantage point.

I said, "I hear it in what she doesn't talk about anymore and in the tiredness of her voice. She calls a lot more often than she used to."

My father said, "I don't like the way he treats her sometimes. You need to keep an eye on that situation."

A chill ran down my spine and I said, "What do you mean?"

Dad said, "Remember when you first met him, and he was asking about her finances?"

"Yeah, I remember," I said. "That bothered me, especially since he asked about that right up front—I think it was only their second date when he brought it up. I thought it was inappropriate, but when I told her about it, she dismissed my concerns."

"Back then, she was driven by loneliness," said Dad. "Your mother is kind of naïve, and she often has too much faith in people." I agreed with him and he said, "I just want you to keep an eye out for signs of trouble, because she is going to need your help."

He was gone as suddenly as he had arrived.

When Felix had inquired about Mom's finances all those years earlier, I had worried about it for months, and then let it go. I figured Mom knew what she was doing with her money.

Finances had never surfaced as a problem with my parents. Dad was disorganized and Mother wasn't, so she took on the bookkeeping duties. She used to spread out her bills on the dining room table while he would sit in his chair, reading. One time while we were living in Afghanistan, he was buried in the latest issue of the *Saturday Evening Post* when she stated, "Fredric, you took some checks out of the checkbook. Do you remember what you wrote them for?"

His head bobbed up, and a guilty look crossed his face. "Umm, let me think."

"Fred, don't tell me you didn't write it down," she scolded. "You know that drives me crazy, because then I don't know what's paid and what isn't."

"I know, hon. Let me get my notebook, and I'll check." Dad got up and went into their bedroom. I sat under the desert cooler—Afghanistan's version of air conditioning. It was beastly hot that day, and I was enjoying the cool, moist air that the ingenious contraption provided. Who would have thought that a large fan and a pipe with holes for water to drip through would be so efficient? It would never work in Delaware or South America with all the humid heat in those places. But here in the desert, it was wonderful.

Dad brought his notebook into the dining room and riffled through it. "Here they are. I did write them down this time." He glared at his notes. He had the worst handwriting in the world and often couldn't read it himself.

Mother said, "Here, let me see if I can figure out what you wrote." She deciphered his code and went on balancing the checkbook. Dad retreated to the living room and his magazine. He looked up just as he started to go back to reading and caught my eye.

"You know," he said, "when you grow up and get married, you want to figure out what each of you is best at and then divide the family jobs between you. I'm terrible at the accounts—as you just saw—so your mom takes care of that."

I nodded that I understood.

"Most men won't let their wives do that, but I know we will have a lot fewer mistakes if your mother manages the finances than if I do. It's just practical for her to take care of it."

I nodded again, and thought about what he had said. "Why won't other men let their wives do it?" I asked. "That's stupid!"

"You're right, but tradition always dictated that the men manage money matters and women the household."

"How old fashioned," I snorted.

"Keep that in mind when you choose a partner," said Dad. "You want a man who isn't insecure and will let you do your share and not relegate you to the kitchen."

Mother chuckled, "If he leaves Nancy in charge of the kitchen, he might just go hungry."

I protested that I could so cook and before I knew it, Dad had maneuvered me into proving it by baking brownies for him. By coincidence, walnuts had just come in with the most recent food shipment from Peshawar.

I knew I was outmatched when he grinned and wiggled his ears at me, so I got up and headed for the kitchen. Dad offered to help, but I saw how tired he looked.

"No, Dad. I'm fine," I said. "You worked hard all day in the heat. You relax. Besides you need to finish that installment of the story in the *Post* so I can read it."

He laughed and went back to his chair and magazine.

I chuckled to myself as I thought of all the tricks he would employ to get me to make brownies or fudge. And Mother always was right in on it.

All these years later I sat in my home office and realized that I would never again see Mother happy like she used to be with her Fred. She had been right: With him she had peace, and she enjoyed none of that now, even though she had found another companion.

Dad's visit made me realize that Mother's situation must be worse than I knew, and I was concerned about the fact that he was worried. I would keep an eye on it and call her more often to see how she was doing. I looked forward to her moving nearby because I could visit with her in person, and I knew this would give her the moral support that she needed as she grew older. On holidays she would be able to come to our busy house and visit with my kids. It would reconnect her life to fun. I hoped it would also give Felix more attention and reduce the pressure between them. Marriage is such a challenging balancing act!

Chapter 25

The Missing Woman

One of the many municipal police departments in the greater Pittsburgh area contacted me about a missing woman. Her mother, Judy, had reported her daughter Claire as missing even though the young woman wasn't living at home. Claire was living in a house with her boyfriend. She had young children that she supposedly had left unattended. Judy had discovered the children alone because one of the older kids called to say they were hungry and their mom wasn't there. Grandma went over right away to find the children with no food and the youngest in dirty diapers. Judy stayed with the children and called the police, insisting that Claire would never have abandoned her kids.

The police found all this to be strange, and so did I. The boyfriend was nowhere to be found; when he turned up later, he told quite a tale of his girlfriend running off with someone else. By that time, Grandma and the children had noticed that Claire's purse was at home and that the covers and bedspread were missing from her bed. Judy and the children had no knowledge of any other man in her life, but all were aware that the boyfriend was frequently violent toward Claire and her kids. Judy was aware that her daughter planned to ask him to leave soon.

I scheduled an appointment with the officers for that evening to review the case.

I usually worked cases in my home office; this time several jurisdictions were involved and we needed a table so we could spread out photos, so we moved into the kitchen. The chief of police handed me a brown envelope full of photos, and I looked through them while the other officers set up microphones and tape recorders.

Among the photos were personal snapshots showing the young mother with her children. I could see in the photos how close-knit the family was. None of the photos gave me any indication that Claire was depressed or suicidal, but in the most recent snapshots, I saw stress and fear in the eyes of the children and the young woman when the boyfriend was also in the photo. None of that showed in the photos that didn't include him. It was also disturbing that the earlier photos of the couple did not show her stress or fear, so what had happened to their relationship to cause such an alteration in the appearance of this family? I described what I was picking up to the officers as I leafed through the photos.

"Did you bring a map of the area with you?" I asked.

The chief slid the map out of an envelope and placed it next to the photos.

I started to verbalize what I was feeling. "To begin with, this young woman would never leave her children unattended. The boyfriend's statement does not fit at all with what I'm picking up. The last thought pattern I get on her is from two days before he said she was gone. It's pretty clear to me that it's not good news.

"They got into an argument because the boyfriend claimed he saw her with another man. That same day, however, her car was in the shop being fixed, and she was home taking care of a sick child. She never left the house at all. As was often the case in their relationship, he wouldn't listen to her."

I paused as I often had to do when the images became severe. By this time in my career, I was used to distancing myself from the pain and emotions of the images I processed. My ability to remain dispassionate engendered respect from the police because I was now reviewing cases with the same professional distance that they had learned to maintain.

I knew the kind of information they would need to prove a case, and

I was busy hunting for it. What evidence was still at the scene that they could use? What mistakes did the boyfriend make that they could capitalize on? What did he use the missing bedding for? Where did he take her body?

We were all working and thinking together to pore through every clue looking for a way to catch this murderer and bring him to justice. My strong focus on gathering evidence helped to deflect the pain and mutilation I was witnessing in the images that flew through my mind's eye.

After a couple of deep breaths, I continued.

"He attacked her and beat her so badly that she lost consciousness. She was lying on the kitchen floor, while he sat at the table and drank beer. He did not call 911 or do anything to help her. Had he called for help at that time, she would have had a chance to live.

"He drank five or six beers before he finally decided to do something. He grabbed a blanket and a sheet from the bed and wrapped her body in them. Blood seeped through so he went back to the bedroom and grabbed the bedspread. Late at night he carried her out of the house over his shoulder and dumped her in the back of his truck, so the children never knew what he had done."

I described the route he took to dump her body. On that trip he passed a little castle. It appeared to be in front of some kind of business, but I could not read the sign. I described in detail what the little castle looked like, including the fact that there was a small cannon in front of it. The description of the castle would turn out to be pivotal in the case.

A few days after the reading I got a call from the chief, "Lady, you are scary!" he said with excitement. "We knew when we were there that you were right about the boyfriend. We were pretty sure that he was lying, but we couldn't prove it.

"We went back to the house and checked the floor of the kitchen with Luminol, and the place lit up. You found the murder scene for us, but he came up with some story to explain why her blood was all over the floor. We needed to find her body.

"Because you were right about the murder scene, we followed your directions and looked for the castle and we found it. I think it used to be a miners' union hall, but there it was plain as day, right down to the stone castle and the little cannon. It sent chills down my spine, I can tell you that. There was a big wooded area across the road. We called for the cadaver dogs and four hours later, we found her. The way he wrapped her preserved evidence, and I am sure he's going away for a long time!"

"I am so glad you found Claire so her family can bury her," I told him. "Thank you for letting me know what happened."

The chief said, "I don't get too many murders in my jurisdiction, but if I get another one, I am calling on you. What you need to know is what I said: you are kind of scary."

I smiled and replied, "I have heard that a time or two."

I savored a moment of success, but wanted to share it with someone. I picked up the phone and called Mother, and together we celebrated that one more killer would not get away! Catching killers is a hard thing to do, but I was used to it now, and it felt good to have a case go through so quickly. Most of my cases took much longer to reach resolution. After I hung up I thought of my dad and how much he enjoyed it when I did something awesome. It felt good.

Chapter 26

Seeing Beyond

One of the difficult aspects of being psychic is that many of the things I can sense about the future are disasters. This is hard to deal with because I want to help people prevent what I see happening, but it's often impossible to do that.

At first when I would see disasters, the images just kept repeating like a nightmare. Each time it repeated, there might be a bit more information than the last time, but still this might not be enough to convince anyone to do anything. I wish I could say that over time things improved and I could use what I receive to help prevent or avoid a large-scale disaster, but that doesn't happen. The first problem is: Who would I go to? The second problem I have found is that no one wants to hear about an impending disaster that is impossible to prevent. And then there is the problem that no one wants to cause a panic of some sort on a *maybe*. Gradually, I have learned to use impending disasters as practice. I work to gather every possible detail so that at least I can share information with friends and family about a threat that might affect us. So, for example, when I sensed that an especially powerful hurricane was going to come inland, we evacuated early so we did not have to leave with everyone else and have trouble finding a safe place to stay. When I work with private clients, the results are better.

When I did a reading for Shannon, a woman who lived in my area, I saw her stopped at a major intersection near Westmoreland Mall in Greensburg, Pennsylvania. She was stopped at the traffic light on an access road to Route 30, the main thoroughfare. I knew that she was coming from a luncheon at the hotel on a nearby hill, a birthday luncheon for one of her friends. The day was cold and windy with snow flurries.

I tried to take in every detail. As she started to cross the intersection I saw a gas tanker run the red light. The truck was going too fast to stop at the light, or the driver was high on something because he blew through the red light and smashed into her. Her small car was totaled, and from the destruction I could see in this wreck, she was unlikely to survive. Flames started coming out of the truck's engine, and I watched the image in horror as the fire caused a full tank of gasoline behind the cab to erupt. If that crash were to happen, I doubted that she or the truck driver would survive, and the explosion would injure people in nearby vehicles.

Shannon had been my client for years, and nothing like this had ever come through before. Without hesitation I told her what I had seen. "I'm sorry to tell you this," I said. "I only tell you so that on the day of the party, you will remember this warning and not enter the intersection. That way the crash won't happen."

Predicting future dangers for clients is a tricky business. When the images take shape in my head, I try to do a rapid calculation to see if there is any way to prevent the occurrence. If I don't see a way to avert it, then I face an ethical dilemma. Should I say anything at all? Telling someone that disaster might strike—a disaster that can't be avoided—can negatively affect the person's remaining life and lead to an unremitting wait for the event to occur.

On the other hand, I've learned that when I do reveal that I see a client face a crash or other peril, the person's knowledge of what is going to happen can save lives. I have known people to survive an accident because I gave a simple warning that it might happen. I have decided that if I am given this kind of information, then I need to transfer it to the person involved. I regard my abilities as a sort of an early warning system, and if I can help someone avoid catastrophe, I will.

When I told Shannon what I saw about the disaster she was headed for, she reacted as expected: the information frightened her. "It's a terrible thing to hear," she murmured. "I know how accurate you are. Is there a way I can avoid the crash? I want to memorize all the details so that I can know when it's going to happen."

I said, "The only way that you can avoid it is not to enter the intersection. When you reach that light, stay where you are. If you do, the truck will blow past." We were both shaken by the images, but she accepted the information and asked a few more questions on how to avoid it.

At the time I made that prediction it was October, and it hadn't snowed. After she left I sat down feeling horrible. Although I knew from past readings it was possible to use images like that to prevent a disaster, I also knew it didn't always work. I remembered a woman I had warned about the mental illness of her boyfriend.

I had done many readings for her before, and she knew I was accurate. I told her, "He is hearing voices and badly needs a psychiatrist. Please try to get him to go to the doctor, and if he refuses you need to stay away from him because I am worried that he will kill you."

"Miss Nancy," she said, "I'm glad you told me this because I've been suspecting that he is having problems, and I've been trying to get him to go to the doctor. Schizophrenia runs in his family, and he won't go to the doctor because he is afraid he has it. I've been trying to figure out what to do, and now I'm determined to get him the help he needs."

"Please don't wait," I urged. "He is very disturbed and I believe he will become violent soon. I know you care about him and you want to get help for him, but don't put that before your safety." I had a horrible feeling when I said goodbye to her that day that I would never see her again. She had been my client for more than 10 years, and we had become friends as well.

I didn't have any more clients coming in that day, so I sat in the sunlight that streamed into my office and tried to deal with what I knew was going to happen. By that time in my career, I understood that it was impossible to change every awful thing I foresaw. The free will of others was still involved, and I had a bad feeling that she would wait too long to act. She was such a kind, caring lady that she would keep trying to help him and put herself at risk.

I think this one hit me hard because I had known her for such a long time and because of the brutality of the attack I saw in my mind. I was used to horrible imagery by now, but I was not usually in a position to try to prevent a murder. I didn't know what more I could do to help her; I had done all that I could. This is one of the hardest parts of being psychic.

I can pick up on disasters in the future—or what we think of as the future. The fact that I had seen events that hadn't yet happened so many times supported what my father had told me—that time is not linear. If it were linear, I couldn't do what I do. I believe that scientists find it handy to explain away the capabilities of competent psychics because it's easier than facing the fact that time is not exactly what people have always believed it to be, so they work hard to deny that someone can accurately predict the future.

I thought about the Garden of Gethsemane and what had happened to me there and the time shift. I thought about some of the times I had been on long drives and thinking hard about something, and then suddenly realized I had arrived at my destination long before it would be physically possible. I had been aware in those instances of some kind of time shift, but I had no idea how that could happen. Gradually, I figured out some of the elements so that I could sometimes recreate the odd shift in time that shortened those long drives.

There were the times that I put my hands on people with broken bones and the bones healed fast. I felt like I had speeded up time, so that made some sense of Dad's claim that time is not linear, and it also explained precognition. If time isn't linear, and I am somehow able to shift my focus and change time, then it would make perfect sense that I could predict the future.

I've done it too many times not to know that somehow I can pick up threads of information about future events. Although it is not always bad news that I sense, it often is disaster that I see. I believe this is because these horrible events are somehow "louder" to me when I am looking ahead. The rest of what I sense that's good news arrives in my mind so softly that it is like a cat on a thick carpet. Little things, like knowing who's on the phone when it rings or thinking of someone I haven't heard from in years and then running into them, come in so quietly I almost miss them. My discussions with professional psychics as well as others with psychic ability confirm to me that our experiences with predictions are similar.

In late November I got a call from Shannon, the client I had warned about the crash with the truck. She was crying so hard I could hardly understand her, causing me to fear that the crash had happened, and she was hurt. I calmed her down enough so she could relate her story.

"You were right, you were right!" she said breathlessly. "He ran that light in front of me! The light turned green and I started to enter the intersection when I heard your voice in my head warning me about this crash. I put my foot on the brake, and the driver behind me had to slam on his. He kept honking for me to go, but I refused to move. And then the tanker blew through the light! If I hadn't heeded your warning, I'd be dead now. Thank you so much for helping me!"

There was a pause and she laughed, "The driver behind me shut up right away!" We laughed together wondering what that driver thought when he saw why she had stopped. My friend continued, "He came to my window, white with shock and asked me, 'How did you know?' I had your card on my center console, and I handed it to him. He read the words and pocketed it. He stayed beside my car for a bit as we were both shaking too much to drive anywhere. The drivers behind him were out of their cars too, all looking our way. It was so weird to know what could have happened, but I was still breathing because of you, Nancy. Consider yourself hugged!"

The news on my other friend was not good. Two months after my warning, I was listening to a newscaster describe the murder of a woman in Pittsburgh. I was only half listening when I heard the reporter say her name. I froze! The TV showed her picture, and the report said that her boyfriend had been arrested for murder. According to his family members, he was mentally ill. I remembered the brutal images I had seen in my mind when I cautioned her, and I mourned my friend and the fact that my warning had not stopped the act of violence that I had seen in her future. The energy drained out of me. I knew my warnings didn't always work, but it was frustrating to know that she suffered so terribly and that she was not able to heed the alert that I gave her. I said a quiet prayer for her soul.

As I sat in my office, I heard Dad clear his throat before I saw him. There he was, on the couch across from me. He said, "You can't save everybody, and you can't solve every case. You tried to help her; she waited too long. She knew you were right, but she couldn't give up on him. I think she didn't believe he would kill her. That was her mistake, not yours."

"Why do I get the impression at all when my warning won't be listened to?" I asked. "Why don't I just get information that potential victims will heed?"

He said, "Each time you get an image like that, you *have* to try to help the person. But people have free will. You never know if you can prevent something. It's just like parents warning teenagers not to drink and drive. They won't always listen."

I said, "It's so frustrating to sit here and watch something horrible in my mind and not be able to do anything about it. I wish I could somehow be more useful."

Dad grew serious. "Here's a mistake you're making. You're forgetting to list in your own mind the many times that you succeeded in changing what you saw in a vision. Don't you remember that pregnant woman and the fence post?"

I had forgotten that one. A client was pregnant and I saw her in a car on I-95 in Delaware between Newark and Wilmington with her husband at the wheel. In my vision I noticed a truck in front of them loaded with metal fence posts. I saw the chains holding the load snap and the posts start sliding off the truck. One long post slid right through their windshield, impaling the woman. Right after I saw that image, I realized the only way she could live was to unbuckle her seat belt and get down on the floorboards. It seemed so illogical to attempt such a maneuver while the crash was happening, but I knew it was the only way she could save herself and her baby.

I said to Dad, "I remember describing everything I could see around her with the hope that she would recognize the situation and save herself when the time came."

He nodded. "She and her baby survived because of your reading. That's what I mean when I say you don't give yourself credit."

"You're right," I allowed, "and yet you're off too. Once I've succeeded in doing it right, I expect it to work that well every time. I guess that's a little unrealistic."

My father said, "Nobody's so perfect that they get it right every time. You need to be fair with yourself if you want to survive this emotionally. You have to deal with so much ugliness in these visions; you have to handle the times it doesn't work the way you want it to."

"I know you're right," I said, "but that lovely lady is dead even though I was able to give her such a clear warning about her boyfriend. I understand it was up to her from that point, but it's frustrating that my efforts to help her failed. I've known her for such a long time, and she was such a kind person. She did not deserve to die that way."

Dad wasn't swayed. "She chose to try to help him even though she knew she was risking her life. It was a sacrifice that she made willingly. In her own way, she was heroic. She gave the gift of her life to try to save his. You need to honor her sacrifice by setting aside your own hurt at losing your friend and remember her and the courage she showed." He disappeared before I could say any more.

I understood what he was saying, but he couldn't fully understand how it made me feel when my efforts to protect someone failed. I was in a down mood, and my mind dwelled on another time when I hadn't been able to save someone.

I had always been fascinated by space exploration. I watched the

Apollo and shuttle launches whenever possible and read up on the astronauts' adventures. I was not surprised when one day I had a horrible image in my mind of a space shuttle launching and then exploding with a force so powerful I knew no one would survive. There wasn't enough information in the vision to place it in time. I did hear a voice saying that some of the metal on the shuttle was substandard. The faulty metal would allow pressurized gas to escape and reach the external fuel tank, contributing to the explosion.

I led a meditation class that night, and I mentioned the vision as an example of how some images, no matter how vivid, fail to provide enough information to do anything with. One of my students asked me a lot of questions about the image I had seen.

"I have a friend who works for a NASA subcontractor," said the student. "I'm taping this, and if it's all right with you, I want to forward the tape to him."

"That would be fine," I said, "but I'll bet it lands in the wastebasket. There isn't enough detail to even figure out what flight it is."

For several classes afterward, my student came in with questions his friend had posed about what I had visualized. Most of the questions appeared to be aimed at identifying the subcontractor who might have produced the poor-quality metal. As far as I know, nothing came from those efforts.

Years later, in 1986, Travis and Heidi were home from school and watching the TV coverage of the Challenger launch when it blew up in front of their eyes. They yelled for me to come and watch because they knew about my interest in space and about my prediction. I watched in shock as the image I had seen years earlier played and replayed on my TV. I had no doubt that this was the explosion I had visualized. As the explosion replayed on the news feed, I remembered every detail of the image I had seen in my mind. It was an exact match. I knew my student who had tried to send the information to NASA would be as upset as I was, but he had only imagined the scene; I had watched it over and over in my mind for years. I could only hope that the information my student passed to his friend would help to unravel the mystery of what had caused this disaster.

Sometimes my predictions averted danger rather spectacularly, as when my client unbuckled her seat belt and slid to the floor boards of the car, saving her life and her unborn child's. Those are the times I try to focus on and celebrate—every unlikely time that I succeeded in helping someone move out of the way of danger.

Chapter 27

Heidi Has Cancer

Heidi and Travis were growing up quickly. At 19 and a good bit taller than I and still growing, Travis had his first car and first job. He loved the independence. Every now and then the little boy he once was peeked out, but most of the time he was a young man and I was proud of him.

By this time Blake had moved to Florida, and I didn't have much contact with him.

Heidi was 15 and in love with figure skating. We had just come back from an international competition in Chicago, which was a lot of fun for us because we got to visit with Susan and her girls. Heidi won some gold and silver medals. She looked lovely out there; at this time in her life, she was happiest gliding around the ice.

I was making dinner when she came into the kitchen looking upset. "Mom, would you please look at this lump on my neck."

I dried my hands and went over to check it. The minute I touched the lump I knew it was cancer, but I struggled not to show my reaction to Heidi. How on earth could she be this sick when she looked so healthy? Maybe it was just a cyst. In my heart I knew it was cancer, and I wanted to reach inside her neck and yank that danger out! I felt rage course through me—Mama Bear rose up, prepared to fight. I tried to cover what I was feeling, but Heidi saw right through me.

"I knew it," she said. "It's cancer, isn't it?"

No matter how tough the news might be, I was always honest with my kids. "I believe that's what it is, but we won't know until you have tests." I wrapped her in my arms and we cried together. I made appointments for her for the next day.

Heidi had had problems the year before this lump appeared when an allergic reaction to a medication damaged her kidneys, which then required surgery. Her doctors were reluctant to put her through another procedure right now, so they recommended that we wait and see what the lump did. This was not acceptable to me—I was determined to get it biopsied right away. I kept pushing the doctors and bringing Heidi in to be checked until they called in a pediatrician to evaluate her. When the pediatrician finished his examination, he sat down with us and said, "Heidi, I think you have Hodgkin's disease. I'm going to order a biopsy right away. This can't wait. The good thing is that I believe you've caught it early, and if I'm right you'll have a 90 percent chance of survival." He abruptly stood up and left the room.

Seconds later, we heard the pediatrician, enraged and screaming at other doctors out in the hallway for missing the diagnosis and wasting valuable time with their wait-and-see plan. Heidi and I sat huddled on the examination table in shock. We were beyond tears.

Weeks of tests followed, each more painful than the last. Finally, Heidi's surgeon called me while I was doing a phone reading to tell me that Heidi did indeed have Hodgkin's. I told my client what was happening and that I was in no shape to continue. She comforted me and agreed that we should reschedule.

After I hung up, I sat in my chair unable to move. Outside was a beautiful day, but the world had stopped for me. I felt my father's arms around me, and he whispered in my ear, "She will survive. It will be hard, but she'll make it."

My daughter's life had already been hard enough; it seemed unfair for her to suffer more. Now I had to tell her that the tests confirmed the Hodgkin's disease without showing my fear, so that she would not be scared. It was an impossible task. I felt my father walking beside me the rest of that awful day and many of the terrible days that followed.

Heidi took the news better than I did. "I knew it was cancer, Mom. I just want to get it yanked as soon as possible."

"Are you sure you understand what I'm telling you?" I asked. Heidi's simplistic view of what awaited her distressed me.

"I understand, Mom. I'm just not going to let it be real in my mind. Let's get this over with." She went upstairs to do her homework. Throughout her ordeal, Heidi refused to acknowledge the cancer. Her oncologist told me that those who survive often react like that, so I followed her lead the best I knew how, which was to be there for her in any way that I could.

Most of the time she had the courage of a lion, but at night she was afraid to go to sleep. I sat with her, night after night, telling her stories about my childhood and what I knew of my parents' childhoods. It kept our minds off the danger and held us together through the nightmare that trapped us. Heidi would finally fall sleep at two in the morning, and I would collapse in sleep until eight when I had to get up and go to work.

The tests she endured were horrible, and we ground our way through it while the doctors tried to determine how far into her body the cancer had spread. She underwent a bone marrow test that went awry. Heidi and I take longer to respond to anesthesia than most people. She was supposed to get her anesthetic shots earlier than usual so they had time to take effect by the start of the procedure. The technicians were distracted and didn't administer the shots on time, despite my reminders. I was sent to the waiting room when the doctor was ready to begin the procedure.

All the way down the hall, I heard Heidi scream in agony. The doctor sent the nurse to get me so I could help Heidi withstand the pain. He had given Heidi more anesthetic, but it hadn't kicked in. I gave her a crash course in Lamaze breathing techniques hoping to reduce her pain, but this wasn't effective.

She gripped my hands and held my gaze as we breathed together. I felt Dad arrive and place his hands on my shoulders. A surge of energy went through me, and that helped to sustain us both. I could feel the energy flow into my arms and through my hands into Heidi. I could tell it was helping because even though she was still in pain, she was calmer. I swore to myself that never again would I let her go through a bone marrow test.

The next ordeal was a laparotomy, an incision that went the entire length of her abdomen. After the doctors opened her up, they checked for cancer and removed her spleen. Her cancer specialist explained that the spleen is like the garbage disposal for the body. Although the loss of this organ would make her more vulnerable to infection, Hodgkin's patients who have the spleen removed face fewer recurrences of the disease down the road. Heidi and I had agreed on this course, as we never wanted to hear the word cancer in relation to her again.

While Heidi was in surgery, I sat in the waiting room with Steve, Travis, and my mother and stepfather. We had been unable to reach Blake in Florida. The operation took forever. Finally, we learned that she had left surgery and was headed for the recovery room. They called us a second time to tell us she was being taken back to her room and we could wait for her there. We were waiting in the corridor outside her hospital room when the gurney transporting her came around the corner. The medical staff pushing Heidi's gurney were talking happily and not keeping an eye on their patient, while I was looking only at her. I could see a slight tinge of blue to the skin around her mouth; the rest of her skin was chalk white. You don't work murder cases without knowing what that means.

Walking behind the gurney was my father. He was carrying Heidi's soul in his arms.

I yelled out loud at the staff to look at Heidi and mentally at my father to give her back to me. I knew her heart wasn't working, that she was dead. I was hysterical, and my mother kept trying to calm me so I wouldn't frighten Heidi. She didn't realize that Heidi was in cardiac arrest—dead, if they didn't succeed in reviving her. The staff rushed Heidi into her hospital room and called code blue.

It was then that Mother realized why I was so upset. To have come through all of this only to lose her now was incomprehensible.

My father walked out of Heidi's room, smiled and winked at me. He was no longer carrying Heidi's soul. In my head I heard him say, "She'll be okay. It was such a joy to hold her. She's so much like you and your mother."

Dad never lied to me, so I knew she would be all right. I had known he would be watching over her during the surgery, but I never expected to see him carrying her. He had mentioned a long time earlier that he was working with children when they passed so they would not be afraid. Was he there to do that for her? Or was he just in the right place when she crossed over and took that moment she went out of body to hold her for a few moments until she could be revived? He never explained, and I didn't think to ask. I was too busy worrying that Heidi might still die.

I felt faint and realized that I had been holding my breath. I took a gulp of air. One of the nurses handed me a box of tissues, and I mopped my tears in vain. The nurse was keeping a close watch on me; I think she was expecting me to collapse. I fought to stay upright.

At last the door to Heidi's room opened; the doctor emerged and opened his mouth to speak to me. I barreled past him to see for myself that Heidi was breathing. He followed me into the room trying to explain what happened. I remember turning on him and saying, "You weren't watching out for her!"

Heidi survived that awful operation and the many rounds of radiation that followed, although she was fortunate not to need chemotherapy. I took her to the rink to ice skate, even when she could barely stand, because it helped her feel healthier. Her friends from her skating team would form a wedge around her and walk with her around the ice to make sure no one ran into her. She could barely make it once around the rink, but she felt more normal on the ice than anywhere else. She figured if I was taking her to the rink, things must be okay, relatively speaking. It was the only fun she had during the entire ordeal.

I can't imagine how hard it must be for parents—who don't have that inner knowledge I have—to see their children go through a critical illness. I knew that Heidi would survive. Even then, as my father warned, it was very, very tough. I was able to trust my instincts and Dad's word, and that made it a little less terrifying. Some days, of course, her condition was so bad that I wondered if she could possibly survive. Nothing is worse than watching your child suffer and not being able to fix it, except losing the child. I've learned from the families of murder victims that that is the ultimate nightmare.

Travis pitched in wherever he could. He helped with the driving, and sometimes he had to carry Heidi because she was too weak to walk. He commented to me, "Mom, she doesn't weigh anything! It's like lifting a pillow. How is she going to survive this?"

"I don't know, Travis," I said as I cried inside, "but I firmly believe that she will."

I remember standing with him in the hallway at the hospital after Heidi nearly passed out during several failed attempts to get an IV line into her frail arms. This was during prep for the surgery to remove the lump from her neck. Travis left the room because he was afraid he was going to strike the technician. I ordered the tech to get someone more experienced to put the IV in just as Heidi refused to let her keep on trying. We learned then that we were dealing with the head of the department, and she insisted on starting the IV herself. The surgeon, a woman, arrived wondering what the hold-up was and sent the lady packing.

She told us, "I'll put her out and then insert the line so she doesn't suffer anymore." The operating room nurse took Heidi away, making sure there were no more botched attempts to put in the IV.

I leaned against the wall, spent with fury that the woman's callousness put Heidi through unnecessary suffering. Travis leaned against the wall next to me. He said, "Mom, I'll never be jealous of Heidi again. This is just too much, and I don't know how she stands it." I was never more proud of him.

On the day we learned that Heidi was in remission, we went out to dinner to celebrate, even though she could hardly eat because her throat was so burned from radiation treatments. She wanted to celebrate and we did. It was the end of an almost two-year ordeal.

Cancer attacks the body, the family, and the soul, but Heidi won.

Chapter 28

Is Blake Dead?

It was one of those crisp, clean fall days. It felt really good to breathe. I had to get to a meeting in Monroeville, Pennsylvania, about 20 miles away from my home in Greensburg, via the Pennsylvania Turnpike, so I was hurrying, trying to gather what I needed and get things at home taken care of in time to make the meeting. I was seat-belted into my car when I realized I had left my briefcase in the house. I barely had time to get to Monroeville on time, and now I had to backtrack.

Twenty minutes later, with the briefcase beside me on the front seat, I went through the toll booth and settled into traffic on the turnpike. I had driven about 10 miles up the road when I realized a very solid passenger sat beside me. I turned, startled to find my son Blake laughing at me. He was still living in Florida at this time, and I hadn't seen him in quite a while, and now here he sat.

I knew he couldn't really be in the car with me, but I didn't think I was hallucinating. My only explanation for his presence was that he was dead. At that thought, I began to sob. I had to pull over to the side of the road because I was blinded by tears. Blake seemed joyous; he kept smiling and waving at me, but he didn't speak. That made me even more fearful that he was dead. I grabbed some tissues from my purse.

I felt my dad's touch on my shoulder, and he whispered in my ear, "He's not dead."

I stared. Blake was still there. If he wasn't dead, how could he be sitting here in my car?

"He's in the Christiana Hospital in Delaware. He's had a stroke," Dad said. Now he was sitting in the backseat of the car, with me and Blake in the front.

"My God," I said aloud. "He's so young! How could he have a stroke?"

Dad said, "He had a bad cold and he took too much cold medicine, which apparently he's allergic to. He went to the ER, but they made him wait, and when he walked over to the nurses' station to get help, he passed out across the desk. He's going to survive, but right now he's not quite himself." Dad reached out to Blake. "He's here, but he isn't able to speak. He can see both of us, and he seems to be able to hear us, but he can't say anything."

Blake looked at Dad and seemed surprised to see him, but I could tell that Blake knew who he was. He shook hands with my father and blew me a kiss as we used to do when he was little, and then he was gone.

"Why isn't he able to speak?" I asked.

"It's the stroke," Dad explained. It's affected his speech, but it's temporary. He's going to be all right. And this just happened, so you won't hear about it right away."

I knew I had to pull myself together to make my meeting. When I arrived I must've looked a mess because one of my friends asked if I was all right. I told her what had just taken place on the turnpike. She helped to calm me down, and then we went to the meeting together.

I can't remember anything that happened in that meeting because all I could see was Blake riding beside me in the car. After he had moved to Florida he would say that when he died, he was going to come back and visit with me because it wouldn't cost any money to do it. He certainly made good on his promise. I just hoped that Dad was right and Blake would be okay.

I thought the meeting would never end, and as soon as it did I called the hospital in Delaware trying to get an update on Blake's condition. A nurse assured me he was fine and put me through to his room. At the sound of his deep voice on the phone, I said, "Blake, how are you?"

"Mom, I had a stroke. Can you believe it?" He sounded so normal.

"No, I can't believe it. Are you going to be okay?"

He said, "The docs did something in my head. They ran all kinds of tests, and they told me I'll be around to drive you nuts for a little longer. How did you know what happened? Dad said he was waiting to tell Heidi until we were sure I was okay."

I told him how he had appeared in my car on the Pennsylvania Turnpike, including how he had shaken hands with my dad.

"That is weird, Mom," Blake said. "I dreamed that I was with you in a car, and I waved at you and you started crying. I tried to tell you I was alive, but you couldn't hear me."

I could hear the excitement in his voice. "So it was real! How cool is that! I mind-traveled, Mom! I always wanted to do that. Wait 'til I tell Heidi. No, you'll have to tell her it really happened because she'll never believe me. I've told her too many stories over the years. I really did it, didn't I?"

"Yes, you did, son. You traveled telepathically. That is amazing!"

He reflected on seeing his grandfather in the car with me. "At first I didn't know who he was. He hadn't visited me since I was a kid," Blake said, "but as soon as he smiled, I knew him. You and your dad have the same smile. I'm glad he was there to help you understand that I was going to be all right."

We talked a while longer, and then he grew tired. I wanted to drive to Delaware, but he didn't want that. He said, "I know you, Mom. You are overworked and you don't need a long drive by yourself. Besides, they're releasing me tomorrow, and I'll be staying with Dad. It will never work to have you two together."

When I got home I called Heidi. I wasn't sure exactly how to tell her what had happened, but I figured the best thing to do was just describe it to the best of my ability. I added that my father insisted Blake was going to be all right. Heidi broke down anyway and said she would call the hospital to talk to him too.

For several days I called Blake and talked to him about his progress. I kept pressing to make the drive to Delaware, but before I could change my work schedule, Blake was released. I had no idea where he had gone and neither did Heidi. All we knew was that he left the hospital with no side effects from the stroke.

What a great relief it was to me that he survived. It was scary that a 21 year old could suffer a stroke. A friend of mine who was a nurse said that the cold medicine he took was being recalled from the market permanently because so many people had experienced allergic reactions to the ingredients. And this was an over-the-counter medicine.

Until we had those phone conversations while he was in the hospital, I didn't realize how much I missed Blake. It was such a relief to know that he was okay. His iron constitution, which had seen him through that reckless childhood, had saved him again.

The whole experience opened up some intriguing issues for me. Blake was alive, yet he appeared as if he were a ghost. I wondered how he did that.

Later Dad would explain, "He was unconscious and actually on the other side when he appeared in the car."

I considered his answer. "So, if you're unconscious and you're on the other side, you can do that?"

"Well," he said, "if you have the right psychic energy you could do that. Apparently Blake has it. I had a talk with him after he left the car, with the idea of helping him reach for a better life. I'm not sure anything I said will get through to him, but I had to try." Dad frowned. "He's quite adept at telling you what he thinks you want to hear. At the time, he means it, but he doesn't seem to have much follow-through."

I said, "Yes, that's a good description of Blake. Maybe this close call will make a difference."

"I don't want you to get your hopes up, Nance," he cautioned. "He's been aimless since he's been living in Florida." Then he smiled. "But as we know, miracles do happen."

Chapter 29
The Whole Strangeness of It

Maybe it has crossed your mind: Is this woman nuts? I've wondered that a time or two myself! I have explained how my mind works, and it seems to be a different process from other people's. As my dad once said and reminded me from time to time, "God just gave you extra gifts. When you're not sure about it and wonder if you're okay, just remember that God made you this way, so He must need you for something important."

Now, with case after case coming at me, I understood better how to use my psychic abilities, but I still wondered why there were so few people who had genuine insights. Year after year I have met people who claimed to be psychic, and I knew they were lying. Every now and then I have met a real one. It's funny in a way, because the ones who aren't real get their claws out the minute they meet me. The real ones, although they're rare, recognize what I am and sit down with me to talk about the ridiculous and funny things that happen to us because people think we know, or should know, everything.

That happened with Illinois psychic and media personality Greta Alexander. We were sitting in the green room of a TV show, *The Other Side*. We started trading stories about the ridiculous things that police had done to test us. We sat together as if we had always known each other, laughing our heads off. Hearing our laughter some of the show's producers and crew crashed the party and sat down to listen to the conversation.

I was telling Greta how the cops I worked with in Wilmington, Delaware thoroughly enjoyed scaring the wits out of new detectives. They had figured out that my attention was instantly attracted to anyone trying to hide thoughts from me, and they told a new detective on the squad about this side of my skills.

This cop was determined to outwit me. He told the other officers he would construct a thick wall in his mind around the thought he most did not want me to uncover. Of course, they all placed bets on this.

When I came in to work the current case, Detective Landon told me, "We've got a new guy, and he is sure he can keep you from reading his mind." He knew me well and understood that I would love the fun of getting through whatever mental defense the new guy had come up with. The officers I usually worked with introduced me to a tall, nice-looking young man, the newest detective. The poor man's upper lip was beaded with sweat, and he looked uneasy.

"What have you been telling this poor young man, guys?" I said to my friends. "He's afraid of me!" They all fell out laughing. From the twinkle in my eyes, they could tell that whatever the young detective was trying to do to block me wasn't working.

"We just told him how good you are, Nance. Nothing unusual."

"Sure you did, and that's why you all bet money." Everybody laughed except this latest victim of dirty-tricks-with-psychics. I looked into this poor man's eyes and said, "Don't worry. I won't tell them about the time you rolled down the hill into the evidence."

His jaw dropped, and he was so unnerved he left the room. Of course his tormentors followed him to figure out what I meant by "the evidence." When they failed to get it out of him, they came back to me.

"Wait a minute!" I protested. "I didn't say I would give *you* the information I read. I just said that I would prove to him his mental defenses don't work against me."

The young man sneaked back to his desk where he sat anxiously watching the veterans interrogating me. I never budged in my position that they didn't have the right to know what he was afraid I would find out. To this day, I have never divulged that the hapless young man fell down a hill headfirst into two badly decomposed bodies.

He did admit to the other detectives that I had instantly homed in on what he was hiding despite the brick wall he had attempted to erect to keep me away from the incident. He was so appreciative of my keeping his secret that he and I went on to work together successfully on many cases. My friends on the police force understood that I try not to intrude on the privacy of people who haven't committed crimes. I don't believe it's ethical to read someone without being invited to do so. But with the young man's admission, they were able to settle their bets.

As we waited in the green room I told a second story about the funniest question ever posed to me. It happened years earlier when I was giving a lecture at a small college in Delaware. The man asking the question was a local farmer who was having a problem with one of his cows.

"She is one of my best milkers," he said. "Otherwise, at this point I'd shoot her out of frustration. She keeps disappearing, and we'll spend hours trying to find her and then she'll just wander in like nothin' happened. Can you tell me where she's going?"

After the audience and I finished laughing, I asked the man, "What is her name?"

"Her name is Henrietta, and she's a darn nuisance. I know she's getting through a fence somewhere, but we can't find a hole anywhere big enough for her to sneak through. If you could even give me a general direction, it would help."

"Do you know where she is right now?" I asked.

"No ma'am, I have no idea where she is."

I had never ranged a cow before, but I figured it wouldn't be that different from ranging a dog, which I had done. As soon as I focused on her name, I felt a breeze caressing her face and could tell she was happy.

"She is standing in a pasture right beside the railroad tracks. There's a nice breeze on her face, and she is waiting for the train. Henrietta loves the whistle of the train. She is sneaking through a narrow space between a gate and fencing. She can get through there because the post holding the gate up is partially rotted and it leans away when she pushes it."

The man exclaimed, "Well, I'll be damned! I know exactly where you're talking about. I'm going to call my son and tell him to go get her."

"The train will come through shortly, and then she'll come home because she needs to be milked," I said.

He shook his head and headed for the entry hall. Laughter followed his exit. I went on answering questions, including a request for help in finding some missing pizza pans. All of a sudden, the farmer was back, shaking his head again.

"Did your son find Henrietta?" I asked.

"He surely did. She was right where you said she was, and she refused to move until the train passed. Stubborn old girl. She's going to end up in the pot yet."

He got a round of applause for his trouble. A month later I got a note from the farmer's wife telling me that her husband now puts Henrietta in the pasture next to the train track every day. He lets her stay there until the train passes, and she's never been missing again.

As I finished telling my stories to Greta and the crew members, we were called back to work, and as we walked on the stage, I heard one of the producers say, "Damn! I should have taken a camera crew down there. That was great footage."

Later that afternoon I sat in the green room thinking. All day I had been getting disturbing vibrations about Greta's health. I had the feeling that she wouldn't be alive much longer. That was a shame. She was one of the kindest people I had ever met.

I sat there quietly thinking about the ongoing struggle: my abilities allow me to know things like this, but I also know when revealing my "vibes" will help and when it won't. As noted earlier, sometimes I have to make ethical judgments about what and how much to tell people. My decision point is whether the knowledge I share will improve or detract from the person's quality of life. I understood that I could not help Greta's health problems.

Greta and I became fast friends because we shared the same ethics, and we were both good at what we did. We talked on the phone often, and we enjoyed having a friend who understood what it was like to be psychic. Greta had a wonderful sense of humor, and we shared a lot of fun together. It was Greta who first dubbed us as "psychic friends," making fun of the many services coming out at that time.

We were thrilled when we were chosen to appear together on a new TV show. Shooting for *The Paranormal Borderline* would take place at the Desilu Productions studios in Culver City, California, in January 1996. That meant Greta, who came from Chicago, and I from Greensburg, would get a vacation from the cold weather while shooting went on. The premise for the show was excellent: actor and director Jonathan Frakes, most famous for his role as Will Ryker in *Star Trek: The Next Generation*, served as host and each week, police departments would bring us unsolved cases, and we would work them right in front of the cameras. The audience would be able to watch us work and then tune in to future episodes to see the results. A big bonus was that Greta and I would have the chance to spend more time together—a rare gift for two psychics not at all used to having friends with equal talents.

On our first trip west, the producers had booked our rooms at a hotel near the studio. When I opened the door to my room, I saw a fruit basket and chocolates, and I was surprised to discover that the room had a loft. I felt like a VIP. They knew how to spoil me and I loved it!

I heard howls of laughter coming from Greta's room down the hall and went to see what was up. I approached her door but had to get out of the way of two men exiting her room carrying a sheet of plywood. The young men were laughing so hard they could hardly carry the board. "What are you doing, Greta? Did you break the room?" I asked.

Greta's daughter had made the trip with her. My friend's health problems were affecting her daily life, but she refused to be deterred from participating in the new show. Now she and her daughter were laughing so hard they couldn't even answer me. Greta's daughter regained her composure first and told me what happened.

183

"Mom went to lie down and hit the mattress with a thud. She thought she was lying on a bed of nails. She nearly fell on the floor because the bed was so hard. I called the front desk and asked for help to get a comfortable one. It turned out some famous producer had the room before us, and apparently he has back problems and needs to sleep on a board."

When we finally stopped laughing, they asked to see my room with the loft. We went back to my room and enjoyed the little sitting area and checked out my fancy basket. Greta's room had a basket too, but with different kinds of goodies. The producers had researched our tastes. Greta's candy was sugar free because she had diabetes. My basket served up an abundance of chocolate and oranges, favorites of mine in those days.

"You know what," Greta said. "I think we've arrived. I feel like a star!"

"I don't know, Greta. You're the one with the bed of nails; I only got a loft!" We started laughing all over again.

That evening as the three of us ate in the hotel dining room, we noticed that a third psychic who would be on the show with us was also having dinner, but she avoided us. I recognized a private investigator I knew from Washington and guessed that he had brought his case down for the show. We had strict instructions not to speak with the police officers ahead of time, and neither Greta nor I would violate that. I waved to him and he smiled and waved back.

Greta and I had crossed several time zones, so we retired early. The producers told us we needed to be up and ready to go early the next morning because they were taking us somewhere special as a surprise.

In the lobby the next morning I found Greta hobbling along in her bedroom slippers. "Can you believe this, Nancy? A star in bedroom slippers! My feet are so swollen, I can't get my shoes on. I hope we're not going anywhere fancy."

The car arrived and I saw the stunned look on our handlers' faces at Greta in bedroom slippers. They packed us in the car and off we went to, of all places, Rodeo Drive, where they had scheduled makeovers for us. What fun!

Greta was mortified but we talked her into going anyway. She was such a good sport. They were supposed to do our hair, nails, and makeup. Greta wouldn't let them touch her hair because she was losing a lot of it, and she was afraid she'd end up bald for the show. One of the ladies at the salon saw Greta's poor feet and suggested that she get a foot massage. Off she went to be spoiled.

The salon owner and his assistant examined me carefully and recommended a trim. I said that was fine but not to color my hair because I might be allergic to the dye. Anyway, I like my hair natural.

"You've never colored your hair?" the young lady asked, in shock. "I have never met anyone with virgin hair! No wonder it looks so healthy!" I had never heard the term "virgin hair" and thought that was funny. I couldn't wait to share it with Greta.

As the stylist started working on my hair, I glanced around the salon. I realized that there was a lot of whispering and staring going on. The women being worked on were all uniformly tanned, manicured, and coiffed. I realized I was among the rich, with their tight jeans, high heels, and jewels. I stared at them while they stared at me.

The young woman in the chair next to me said, "Did you-all win a makeover?" I knew by her tone she intended to put me in my place.

I heard my father's calming voice. "Don't rise to the bait, Nance. She's a trophy wife and she's insecure."

"No," I said patiently. "We're psychics who are making a new TV show called *The Paranormal Borderline*."

The young lady gasped and instantly forgot her effort to establish turf. She started firing questions at me, as did some of the other customers. The stylists had frozen when the young woman started in on me. Now they stifled giggles at how my answer had turned the tables. Thank goodness my father spoke up, or I might have lost my temper and that is never good, especially on Rodeo Drive.

By the time my hair was cut, the customers were deciding whether they liked my hairstyle and acting like my new best friends. The young ladies working on me loved it. When Greta came out, I introduced her and everyone made a big fuss over her too, even suggesting some tea that might help with the swelling in her feet. People are funny.

Greta and I worked well together and kept coming up with accurate reads that would be confirmed the following week. It was great fun collaborating with her and having the chance to show our work as it was happening. No fuss; just good old quality work.

The Paranormal Borderline was just starting to catch on when the network canceled it in May 1996 after nine episodes. They had scheduled us against *Frasier*, and we had no chance against NBC's blockbuster sitcom. To this day I still meet fans who wonder why we went off the air because the show was so wonderful.

Before the show ended, host Jonathan Frakes sent Heidi some photos from *Star Trek: The Next Generation*. The crew had told him that she was a "trekkie"—and a cancer survivor. Frakes said he wanted to give her the photos because he admired her courage.

Not long after the last show wrapped, I heard that Greta had died. I miss having a friend so much like me.

Chapter 30

Heart Attack

Mom and Felix moved to a retirement community north of Pittsburgh and about an hour and a half away from my home in Greensburg. It was the summer of 1996, and Mother was now 79 years old. Mother and Felix seemed be doing better since Dad had warned me about the difficulties in their marriage. I was glad that they were now closer to my home, as I had become even more aware of Mother's infirmities and could at least give her better emotional and physical support. Aging was proving difficult for both Mom and Felix, and it was clear that her thinking was affected. She had not looked well lately, and she seemed unhappy. I hadn't been sure if her growing frailness was physical or emotional.

One night Felix called me from Passavant Hospital not far from their home. They were at the emergency room because Mother had collapsed at home—maybe something to do with her heart, he said.

Luckily Travis was at home, and we picked up Heidi at her grocery store job and headed for the hospital. On the trip, Travis sat silently beside me. He now stood 6 feet, 5 inches tall. He had a job, but I was glad he had been home when the call came from Felix. Usually he was out with his friends. Heidi sat silently in the back seat. Steve and I had divorced almost three years earlier, and it was just the three of us at home now.

There was no time to try to reach Blake in Florida, and I really didn't know where he was anyway. I would try to reach out to him once I knew what was going on with Mother.

"You want me to drive, Mom?" Travis asked.

"That's okay, Travis. Thank you for offering, but it will help me to have something to focus on." This was the first time something this serious had happened to Travis and Heidi's precious grandmother, and I had seen the shock in their faces. I had driven before under such stress; Travis had not. The trip to the hospital required more than an hour of driving, first on the turnpike and then on winding country roads with no lighting. It was a moonless night, and I had to watch out for the deer that are so prevalent in western Pennsylvania.

I glanced into the rearview mirror at Heidi in the back seat. She was white and her face tense. She saw me looking at her, and she looked away but not fast enough for me to miss that she was fighting tears. I put my attention on the basics of driving. Travis had the directions to the hospital, and Heidi was watching for road signs. It kept us all from thinking too much.

At the ER the kids stayed in the waiting area, and I went back to see Mom.

She was alone with a burly male nurse. When I walked in, he said, "Your mom said you'd be here soon." He motioned for me to come closer.

I didn't realize that I had stopped just inside the curtain. Mother looked awful. I could see the vein structure under her translucent, colorless skin. Until she turned to look at me, I had thought she was dead.

The nurse said loudly, "I'll be back to check on you, Harriet. No dancing now, you hear?" Then he left us alone.

A faint smile crossed my mother's mouth, but it didn't show in her eyes. She was afraid, and when I put my hand in hers, she clung to it. I had never seen her frightened like this. I moved to sit beside her before my legs gave out on me.

"He wouldn't call the doctor," she whispered.

I was startled. "What? Why wouldn't the nurse call the doctor?" I started to get up. "I'll call the doctor."

She continued to hold my hand. "Not the nurse. Felix. I was lying on the floor. I couldn't get up, and I asked him over and over to call the doctor and he wouldn't do it. I finally shouted at him to do it, and then he did."

She burst into tears. I held her while she cried. I had no idea what to think. Was Felix in shock? He had shown before that he could not act in difficult situations.

I asked, "Do you think he froze?"

She thought about it. "No, he just wouldn't get help." We sat in silence until the nurse returned.

"Harriet, how are you feeling?" asked the nurse as he checked her monitor. He turned to me and asked, "Are you her daughter?"

"Yes, I'm her youngest."

"The doctor would like to talk to you. He's down to the right. I'll take care of your mom while you talk with him."

I kissed Mother and told her I would be right back.

I walked up to a group of doctors who were conversing in a huddle. "I'm Harriet Dankowski's daughter. Did one of you want to speak with me?" They all turned. The tallest was wearing scrubs. He motioned for me to come with him and took me to a private room.

"Your mother has several blockages and is in danger. She needs to have surgery."

"Tonight?" I asked.

"No," he answered. "We want to get her stabilized, and we need to run some more tests. Right now early tests are coming back with consistent results indicating an imminent heart episode." The doctor added, "We are still waiting for some results."

I tried to absorb what he was saying.

The doctor said, "Mrs. Dankowski says that her husband refused to call for help. Did she tell you that?"

I was surprised that she had told the doctor. Mother was extremely private about things like that. "Yes, she did."

"Do you think she's telling the truth?"

"Yes, I do," I answered. "I've seen some problems with him over the years. He has a terrible temper, and they haven't been getting along. Maybe he just froze; he does that under stress."

The doctor paused. "Yes, well, shock can be a hard thing to function under for some people. Maybe that's it." Then he asked, "You are your mother's blood daughter? Or are you Mr. Dankowski's daughter?"

"Felix is my stepfather. My father died of a heart attack years ago," I explained.

"I see," he said. "That makes this situation harder for you, I'm sure. Who has the power of attorney for your mother?"

It suddenly dawned on me why the question about whether I was her blood daughter. I asked if Felix was not cooperating in her treatment.

The doctor went on to tell me that Felix was having difficulty making decisions about his wife's care, and the hospital needed to understand the legal situation. I was stunned when he told me that Felix said he had sole power of attorney.

"No, that's not true," I stated firmly. "She gave us both power of attorney,"

He seemed surprised, and asked, "You wouldn't happen to know how it's worded would you? Is it either-or?"

"Yes," I said.

As he scribbled notes on the chart, I told him the document that we all signed was at the retirement community, and I offered to retrieve it. He said the hospital would take care of that and suggested that I stay with Mother. He arose and told me he would continue to monitor the test results and complete the paperwork that would result in her admission to the cardiac unit.

I had thought it odd that Felix wasn't here with Mom, and I asked if the doctor knew where he was.

He said as he leafed through his papers, "I think someone from social services is meeting with him. I'll see you back in Mrs. Dankowski's room."

What on earth was going on? Was he refusing all treatment for Mom?

By the time I got back to her, Felix had returned and now sat beside her, but they weren't talking. When I walked in he jumped up. "You sit here with your mother," he offered. "She needs you."

He moved away and I could tell he was relieved. What on earth was the matter with him? I reached for Mother's hand, and she gripped me weakly. She was dozing so I sat quietly beside her.

One of the nurses brought Felix a chair, but he waved it off. "I think I'll go down to the cafeteria and have dinner. I'm hungry." I sensed that Felix wanted to get out of the room because he couldn't face Mother. I didn't want to think he would deliberately refuse treatment for his wife, but that seemed to be the case. Perhaps he *was* in shock.

After he left the room, Mother whispered, "He's not hungry. We ate before this happened. He just can't face me." Her words confirmed what I had sensed in him. She paused, perhaps thinking about his failure to help. "Why would he do that?"

"I don't know, Mom, but you need to not worry. Felix and I will look out for you now." I wondered too, why would he do that?

She opened her eyes, glared at me, and said with her tone firmer, "You look out for me. After what he just did, I don't trust him."

I smiled. "Don't worry, I'll stay here. You just rest." She fell asleep. Had Felix just frozen or was there something sinister about his behavior? I was dozing in my chair when I felt Dad's hand on my shoulder. He said softly, "Be sure you are here early tomorrow. Felix is not able to handle this and won't do what's right for your mother." He paused and added, "Make sure you have the power of attorney document with you."

Dad's presence had sharpened my senses and I looked around for him, but he was gone. I could feel the calmness he always conveyed and his love surrounding us.

I wanted to stay in the ER with Mother, but I knew that Travis and Heidi would be anxious for news. I found them in the waiting room and filled them in on Mother's condition and the problems with Felix. Fearful to leave before we could be sure Mother was safe, the three of us waited until Felix had gone and Mother was settled in for the night. Finally, I made the long drive home with my children, both asleep in the car. My father was with us. He sat in the back seat next to Heidi and gave me strength as he helped me to watch out for hazards on the dark, winding Pennsylvania roads.

I was awakened early the next morning by the insistent ring of the phone. It was Mother's cardiologist, who said, "Your mother is scheduled for surgery today. We've arranged to have a team from Mercy Hospital do it. Is that all right with you?"

I cleared my groggy brain. I told him that I needed his assurance that they could handle the job.

"Yes," he said, "they are excellent, which is why I want them to do the surgery. They'll operate this afternoon, but I will need to meet with you and your father this morning."

"Stepfather," I corrected. "My father is deceased."

"Sorry; stepfather. I just need you to be present so there will be no problems or misunderstandings."

Now I was wide awake. It sounded like Felix still wasn't cooperating. I had to get ready in a hurry to rush to the hospital. I had called Susan the night before, and she was on the way from Illinois.

At the hospital the doctor explained to Felix and me what was going to happen: "We have identified five major blockages, all of them serious. Harriet needs to have bypass surgery right away—this afternoon."

"No!" Felix blurted out. "I won't allow it."

"He's a little hard of hearing," I said to the cardiologist. "Maybe he didn't understand. Can you explain it again?"

The doctor went through the explanation again, only louder this time.

Felix smiled in the strangest way and said, "I heard you the first time. I just won't allow it. She is not having this surgery."

He had lost his hold on reality, and my dad's words from the previous day came back to me: "Felix is not able to handle this and won't do what's right for your mother."

The doctor turned to me and asked, "I understand that you are equal in the power of attorney, is that right?"

"Yes, I am," I answered. Thanks to Dad's warning, I had slipped my copy of the power of attorney document into my purse before starting out for the hospital.

Felix exploded in rage. "She is nothing! I'm Harriet's husband! You have to do what I want, and I don't want the surgery!"

The doctor turned to me for clarification, and I handed him the power of attorney document, and he read it while Felix continued to threaten us.

The doctor said to Felix, "Sir, it is clear from this document that Nancy has equal authority in this matter." He turned to me and asked, "Do you authorize this surgery to be done?"

"Yes, I do," I said. "How soon can you do it?"

Felix's fists were balled up, and I was afraid he would attack us. The doctor ordered him to sit down and stop threatening us, or he would have Security remove him. He quieted, but I felt him seething with rage. I signed the permission form for the surgery and then left. I went back to the waiting room to find that Susan had arrived. Felix stormed in behind me. He blocked the door of the waiting area and started raging at both of us, fists raised. Most of what he said was incoherent, but Susan and I found it terrifying.

Finally a man wearing a white coat came by in the hall and asked if we were all right. I don't know if he was a doctor or an administrator, but I could tell that he had heard the commotion and come to see what was going on.

By this time Susan and I were shaking, and when the man moved Felix away from the door, we hurried into the ladies room. Now we knew what Mother meant when she talked about Felix yelling and behaving in a frightening manner.

Finally, Mother's doctor came in with the team from Mercy Hospital, and they filled us in on what to expect. They decided to postpone surgery until the next day, as they wanted to give Mother more time to stabilize.

In bed that night I prayed. As I started to fall into a bone-weary sleep, I heard my father's voice, "Your mother is going to survive the surgery, but she'll need your help afterward. She will have a difficult time with her recovery and with Felix."

It was a comfort to me to know she would pull through, but through my haze of exhaustion, I didn't want to think about what might happen afterward.

The surgery seemed to take forever. When Susan and I were able to see her in the recovery room, I thought she couldn't possibly survive; she looked that terrible. As I stroked her cheek, one of the few places without tubes, I saw a tear trickle from her eye. She was unconscious, but I felt she knew I was there. We were allowed to be with her only a few minutes at a time, but the nurses assured us she was doing fine. The operation was a success.

Mother was incredibly frail and now with the problems that Felix had caused, would she choose not to come back from the edge of death? As I processed this thought, there was my father's hand on my shoulder again. That steady strength flowed through me and helped me to stand up to the stress of this ordeal for Mother's sake, but I had no idea what to do about Felix.

As I sat there with my sister, watching our mother, I thought how different Mom's life would have been if her beloved Fred had lived. She would not have had to struggle so hard just to survive. I knew all three Myer women judged men by the standards Dad set: What we knew of men, he had taught us. Mother used to get testy from time to time. Dad always knew that was a sign of stress; he never took it personally. Instead, he would reach for the nearest tissue box and say, "Harriet, you need a good cry. Here's some tissue. Go ahead and cry."

He would wrap his arms around her, and she would finally be able to let her emotions go. After the storm passed, he would help her work through what was bothering her. They did everything together, so unlike what I saw in other marriages I witnessed over the years, including my own.

Three days after surgery Mother was moved out of ICU into a private room. She was exhausted and in a lot of pain, but I could see her relief at being surrounded by her daughters and grandchildren. We all took turns visiting and encouraging her just by being in the room with her. We knew she was too tired for conversation; she just needed to see a loving face. She had had a bad reaction to the anesthetic used during surgery; it made her confused to the point that she began to feel she wasn't safe at the hospital. I arrived on her floor to have the nurses tell me she had been threatening them all day with—of all things—me.

"Your mother says you have a lot of police friends," one of the nurses said, "and that you are going to get us all in trouble."

"Oh, she does, does she?" I returned. "And what did you do to make her threaten you like that?"

The nurse explained, "She had to have blood work today, and she was upset because it hurt so she told us all off."

I smiled. "I guess in some way that must mean she's getting better."

"Oh, yes," said the nurse. "She is quite the queen bee today."

I stuck my head in Mother's room to be greeted abruptly. "Where have you been? I've been trying to get these people to call you. They aren't treating me right, and you are the one to straighten them out!"

"I'm glad to see you are getting better, Mom. How have they been treating you badly?"

She showed me her arms. "Look at all these bruises," she exclaimed. "They must have been beating me. Can't you do anything?" I handed her the tissue box and sat on the bed holding her as she wept. She said, "I wish your father were here. He'd know what to do." She wiped her eyes and leaned against me.

"Well, at least he left me behind to help you," I said. "You've just had major bypass surgery. That's where all the bruises came from. They are taking very good care of you. It's just that the drugs they used have confused you a bit."

She admitted to feeling confused and asked again, "Why did they operate on me?"

For the rest of the first week, I had to go over what happened many times until she began to remember again. She continued to improve physically, but the drugs and hours on a bypass machine had mixed her up terribly. She just didn't feel safe anymore. How I wished that my father—alive and strong—could be here to comfort her. I knew where the fear came from, but at the moment she didn't seem to remember what Felix had done, or rather, refused to do, and it could only frighten her more if I reminded her of it. I took time off from consulting with my clients and stayed with her in the room at night so she would feel safer.

In the second week she calmed down enough that I didn't have to sleep in her room. Shortly thereafter, she was able to go back to her home in the retirement community. She had survived quintuple bypass surgery, but now she had to complete the long road to recovery that all members of the "zipper club" face.

Chapter 31
Lady's Gift

For several years I lived with a wonderful rescue dog named Lady. She was a blonde Labrador retriever and the most loving animal imaginable. At some point before she was rescued, she must have gone through extensive training in helping a handicapped person. I had figured this out the first night I had her, because I dropped the phone and she got up, came over, picked it up, and handed it to me. It was quite a surprise.

That first night when I went to bed, I put a nice quilt outside my bedroom door for her and patted it so she would understand it was for her to sleep on. After giving me a big kiss, she curled up on it and fell asleep. I went through my routine of getting ready for bed and then settled down under the covers with a book. As soon as I was in bed, Lady rose from her quilt and walked into my room. I was shocked when she lifted her nose to turn off the light. Then she walked softly back to her bed.

What kind of dog turns out the light?

The next morning I took Lady outside. Barbara, my landlady, had convinced me to go with her to the animal shelter in the first place and was excited to see how the two of us were getting along. I recounted the story of Lady retrieving the dropped phone.

"She must have been trained!" said Barbara, who proceeded to give Lady commands, and the dog responded to every last one of them. "Extremely well trained," said Barbara. "She knows every command I know!"

I didn't know any, and it took weeks of studying a book of standard commands for me to learn to communicate with Lady. In the meantime she did her best to overcome the language barrier. She adored me, and soon the feeling was mutual. When we went for walks, she would guide me away from anything she perceived as danger, whether it was a garter snake, a deer behind a tree, or a hole she saw that I didn't. She used the kind of moves I had seen guide dogs use.

After a while I moved to a new house with a big yard and a field behind the house, where Lady and I enjoyed long walks. She was so well trained that I did not have to keep her leashed in this rural setting. She was a great companion even though she did snore rather loudly, and her calm nature was a great help to me as I adjusted to my empty nest. Heidi and Travis were out on their own, and I was living alone.

Late one night I finished watching the news and let Lady out before going to bed. I had gotten into the habit of carrying my cell phone with me because I had worked too many cases where women who lived alone were attacked at night. I was standing near the porch admiring the stars, and Lady was off taking care of business when I felt a hostile presence watching me.

My skin crawled with a sense of danger. I called Lady but she was occupied and could not respond right away. My landlord was a dentist, and his office was no more than 20 feet away from my porch. Suddenly, I saw a man walk down the steps of the dentist's office. The stranger had been sitting in the shadows watching me. All the warning bells in my brain went off. This man was dangerous, and I had no illusion about what he wanted.

I pulled out my cell phone and backed toward the door of the house as I dialed 911. Lady whined softly so I knew she sensed that something was wrong. The gentle pressure of my father's hand touched my left shoulder and his voice told me, "Whatever you do, don't show fear to this man. He thrives on it. Act like he doesn't threaten you at all."

From where the man was coming, he could not see Lady. I knew that she was about to become a nasty surprise to him.

I stammered into my phone, "There's a man coming at me from the dentist's office on 981. My house is on Monastery," and I gave the number. Then to the prowler I said: "Sir, you need to stop where you are. My dog is right here, and he'll attack you if you come any closer." I figured it would be better if he thought Lady was a male dog.

"Is he stopping?" I heard the 911 operator ask.

I exclaimed, "Sir, do not come any closer or my dog will attack you!" I hoped the operator understood.

The operator said, "Troopers are on their way, miss. Can you get inside the house?" Now the stranger spoke. He said, "I'm just waiting for my sister. I won't hurt you."

I warned him again, but no matter what I said, he kept creeping toward me. "My sister lives right there," he said calmly. "I'm just waiting to see her. I just want to chat with you."

Lady trotted out of the shadows where she had been and stood between me and the stranger. Suddenly, she let out the most ferocious growl I had ever heard. She sounded like a lion.

I backed up on the porch and was now standing with my back against the kitchen door.

He had finally gotten a good look at the size of Lady, and he stopped as if he realized she really might attack him. She continued to snarl and growl at him, sounding like an absolute beast. I couldn't believe it was my gentle dog.

The man wasn't giving up yet, but Lady's growls gave him pause. Just then I heard sirens closing in on my house. The man still didn't move, but by now I had the door open as I tried to back into the house. I called Lady, but she refused to budge. The hair on her back was up, and she continued her guttural growls. She sensed, as I did, that he was still going to attack.

The troopers arrived together. One car swung in the driveway behind me. The other pulled into the dentist's parking lot, in front of me but behind the stranger. The troopers unloaded quickly with their guns drawn. Lady paid no mind to the troopers; she knew they were friendly. She stood her ground in front of that man and snarled like a lion. The troopers closed in on the man, and he put his hands up. The stranger became Mr.

Cooperation all of a sudden, a real smooth talker.

Lady backed up onto the porch; she was not off-duty yet as growls rumbled through her. It was a shock to me how seriously she defended me because everything I had read about Labradors indicated that they weren't good guard dogs. I had no doubt that Lady had just saved my life.

The troopers escorted the stranger to a semi parked on the other side of the road. I had seen that truck parked over there for the past three nights and wondered about it, but this was the first time I saw him. The officers watched him leave, and then they came over to take my statement.

"Miss, we're sure that man was up to something bad, but we don't have anything we can hold him on at this time. He claims he was waiting for his sister, and he's sorry he scared you."

"Right," I stammered. "He claims his sister lives in the house on the corner? That's a real estate office, not a home. And he kept coming at me after I told him to stop, and he wouldn't have stopped if Lady hadn't been here."

One of the officers said, "That's one amazing dog you have there! When I came around your house and saw this blonde shape growling like a lion, I didn't know what I was up against."

Lady walked over to the trooper and sat down to be patted. He wasn't sure what to do. "I take her to visit people as a therapy dog," I said. "She's expecting you to give her a pat."

Hesitantly, the trooper reached out and patted her big head, "You deserve some pretty big pats tonight for saving your mistress." Lady just sat there contentedly.

The troopers left saying, "We told him to stay away from your house. You see that truck again, you call us immediately. I think we all agree he's not a safe man."

Years later, I was watching a news report about a serial killer who had just been arrested. He was a trucker, and he traveled up and down the east coast and killed in many states from New Jersey to Pennsylvania and on up north. The minute they showed his face, I recognized him. It was the stranger that Lady had protected me from. I knew I had been in danger that night—my own senses, my father's instructions, and Lady's reaction all told me so. But I had never realized how close to death I had come. The man sweet-talked the women he killed so that he could get close to them. He carried a kill kit and put them through a nightmare of torture. Thank God for my psychic ability and Lady, or I wouldn't be here.

Chapter 32
Hirosaki

I was invited to do a TV show in Japan, a country I had always wanted to visit, but an opportunity had never presented itself. It was a little intimidating going almost halfway around the world alone, but I'm an adventurer at heart.

Flights back and forth to Japan are long—12 to 13 hours to get there and 11.5 hours back. When I arrived in Tokyo, a video crew and a translator met me at Narita International Airport. I worked on some cases on location with this local crew, then flew back to the United States, only to return two weeks later to film the second part of the show on a set in front of an audience. This became my routine for the next four years.

During one of those trips I was sent with the crew to Hirosaki in the winter. Hirosaki is a city on the northern end of Honshu, the largest island in Japan. We traveled icy roads on a large bus, which slid and skidded multiple times during the trip. I was the only passenger awake to know that, as the Japanese seem to have an amazing gift for falling asleep on public transportation almost as soon as they sit down. And then somehow they know exactly when to wake up.

We went to the scene of a horrible arson in a building that had housed offices and a daycare center. The fires were set in a way intended to trap the maximum number of people. Many people were killed and injured, and the building was destroyed. The ruins of it had since been torn down—the location was now an empty lot covered with grass. I could sense where the building's stairwells had been and knew that the killer had set fires at each stairwell to keep people from escaping the building. The man had had a conflict with the company located in the top-floor offices, and he planned to get even—with no concern for the small children in the daycare center and all the others working in the building.

Bundled against the cold and the bitter wind, I paced back and forth across the empty lot. I described the arsonist and how he had gone about setting the fires. Although I stood on a vacant lot, I was seeing the former building and could point out each area where a fire had been set. The film crew had visited the burned-out building prior to its demolition, and they were astounded to see me walking around within the areas of the building and accurately identifying the points of origin of the fires.

After we left the scene, I tried to track the killer. It was confusing for me because his thoughts were in Japanese, a language I don't speak. I could only depend on the images in his mind. I directed the crew to take me from place to place where I was sure he had been. The locations seemed random, and I couldn't make sense out of why the perpetrator had moved all over the area.

I began to doubt myself because what I tracked seemed so illogical. I was jet lagged and exhausted—could that account for perceptions that seemed so inaccurate? As the Japanese crew patiently drove from one place to the next and I struggled to figure out what was going on, I heard my father's voice. "You are correct," he reassured me. "Even though it doesn't make sense to you, the information you're giving them is right." I took a breath and kept directing the crew to meander through different stops.

We ran out of time for any more shooting, and the crew and I returned to Tokyo. I worked with a Japanese artist the show's producers hired to draw a portrait of the arsonist. I had worked with this artist before, and he was quite good once he got used to drawing from only my description and not referring to a model. In addition, the language barrier required us to work through a translator. Despite these challenges, I knew when he showed me the drawing that it was accurate.

When I finished this stint on the show, I returned to the United States. Two weeks later I was back in Japan to do the portion of the show in front of the audience. The producers were excited because they already had evidence that the portrait I had helped to create was accurate. A few weeks after that, the segment aired on television.

I was back home again when the show's director contacted me, thrilled to give me some news. Twenty-four hours after the program had aired revealing the information I uncovered and showing the composite portrait, the arsonist was arrested! After his arrest he confessed. Why had I followed him all over the city? Because he was a taxi driver. This case was a new record—24 hours to arrest, beating my previous record of one week from reading to arrest.

Chapter 33
The Struggle

I wish that I could say that Mother recovered completely from her heart surgery, but she didn't. Her body bounced back well enough, but she had a lot of trouble with forgetfulness and depression. Felix's lack of response to her emergency left her feeling unsafe.

In my opinion Felix also suffered from depression, which I trace back to a stock market drop that cost him all his assets. Mother's holdings withstood the drop, but his were wiped out. He changed a lot after that and was constantly feeling threatened and fearful. I think he was afraid he would lose his home. He couldn't grasp that Mother would never think to throw him out on the street because of the financial loss he had suffered. She had enough money to take care of both of them.

The confrontation at the hospital over Mother's surgery created additional problems between us. It all made for a sad situation for both of them. My home was a long drive away, so I could not be there every day. I visited as often as possible to keep them in touch with people and to help them function as well as they could. It was a rough introduction for me to the harshness of aging—seeing intelligent, interesting people descend into a fearful, anxious state with no sense of security.

Mother also began to lose the use of her hands. She often suffered painful cramps in them, and her fingers curled into an involuntary claw-like position. She could not paint anymore; that loss broke her spirit, as painting was her refuge.

Mother suffered some strokes that further impaired her thinking, but she always knew who I was, and we giggled and chatted during our visits. I wanted her to feel that she could always count on me, and she let me know she appreciated it. By this time she had moved to a dementia ward in a nursing center. I wanted to have her tested to make sure she actually suffered from dementia or Alzheimer's and not something else that could create similar symptoms. Susan and I thought Mother was too lucid to belong in a dementia unit, yet it was clear she needed assistance.

During discussions of Mother's care and treatment, Felix, also living at the center, lost control and attacked a social worker, demonstrating that something serious was wrong with him as well. In a move I didn't understand then and still don't, the care center decided to place mother in the locked unit, supposedly so she could be protected from Felix's temper. Punish the victim for the aggressor's lack of control? All I could do was make sure I was there every week to comfort her.

On one of my visits I learned quite by accident that Felix was seriously ill with heart problems. No one had said anything to Mother or me, but it was lucky that I found out because now I could take more of a lead in her care. They still refused to test her to make sure that she really had Alzheimer's. I was exposed every week to people with that awful disease, and there was a steady decline in their cognitive functions. Occasionally, they experienced a day of lucidity. Mother's problems were different. She did not go straight downhill, but swung back and forth from clarity to a fog. I noticed she was always worse when she did not eat well. Her depression fluctuated in a similar pattern.

Mother finally overheard some nurses talking about Felix, and when I arrived to visit her she informed me that the nurses said he was dying. She was upset that no one told her, and she wanted to visit him. I talked with the head nurse, who initially refused to give me any information. I pointed out that according to the guardianship papers, once Felix became incapacitated I became Mother's full guardian. She admitted that she was aware of that, but she hadn't been allowed to tell me about his condition.

Felix was dying of heart failure and had been cared for on the nursing unit for some time. Mother's nurses advised me that I should not take her to see him because he was subject to fits of rage. I found his deterioration so sad—he had been a brilliant man at one time with a Ph.D in chemistry. Old age was not kind to him.

A few weeks later Felix died, and Mother had to go through the trauma of surviving a second husband. At least it simplified her care as I was now her only guardian.

Not long after Felix's death Mother ended up in the hospital again—this time with internal bleeding. The nursing care center had delayed getting her to the hospital when the bleeding started, and they had not informed me about her condition. This was the last straw and upon her release from the hospital, I moved her to a different care center 10 minutes from my house. It took Mother a long time to trust the staff at the new care center.

I had discovered in a very painful way that the quality of care a resident of a nursing home receives can have a lot to do with how often relatives check in. Mother's new care home, Spring Gardens, was a big improvement. She was treated like a person, not a body. The attitude difference was not lost on her.

"I like this place," she said many times. "They are nice to me here."

As she recovered from the injuries that had put her in the hospital, she started to come out of her shell and returned to the forceful person she once had been. It was amazing to see this personality reappear; it had been missing for so long—for years.

"You know," she told me. "I'm not as stupid as they think I am."

I said, "They don't think you're stupid, Mom. They can see you're getting better all the time."

"That's right. I *am* getting better, and I'm not going to put up with being in here with these crazies."

"Oh boy," I thought. She had been placed in their dementia ward upon arrival because she had been so ill and confused. But as she improved and underwent blood tests—which I had insisted on because the internal bleeding she suffered had taken some time to stop—her doctor discovered that Mother had pernicious anemia, not Alzheimer's. Pernicious anemia occurred in her case because she was missing something called the intrinsic factor in her blood. It was a genetic disorder and completely treatable. Her doctor ordered immediate vitamin B-12 shots.

The day after her first shot I walked into the unit to find Mother staring at her hands in amazement.

"Look at this," she said. She held up her hands, and her fingers were long and straight—no longer in a lobster-claw position. She wiggled her fingers at me and smiled a wonderful, triumphant smile. "And you know what else I can do?"

"I'm almost afraid to ask," I said as I sat down beside her.

"I can think straight. You're Nancy, and I know that."

She fixed a level gaze on me and said, "Now, get me out of here." Then she grinned—her most mischievous grin, which I had not seen in years. Her eyes sparkled and she glowed.

I was amazed at her improvement from just one shot administered less than 24 hours earlier. Inside I also was furious that this deficiency had not been diagnosed and treated a long time ago.

"It's nice outside," I remarked. "Would you like to take a stroll around the place?"

"Didn't I say get me out of here?" She laughed and undid her wheelchair brakes. Off we went tooling around while she greeted all the people she knew by name and said hello to everyone else. The staff was as surprised as I was by the change in her. She was so much more normal now; of course, that also meant she was a force to be reckoned with—not an easy task.

After I tucked her into bed that night, I sat in my car and thought. This problem was something she had been born with. Her doctor told me that the stress of the open-heart surgery probably had halted her minimal ability to process vitamin B-12, and without the monthly supplemental shots, she would deteriorate in many ways, including mentally. B-12 is that critical to the survival of the human body, especially the nervous system, and deficiency can cause strokes if left untreated. Each of the several strokes she suffered before the B-12 deficiency was diagnosed damaged her thinking a little more.

All this time, my sister and I had been trying to get her doctors to run a full battery of tests because Mother did not act like the other Alzheimer's patients. The first care home had flat out refused to run the tests, and now we knew that she would never have been on a dementia ward if she had been receiving proper medical care. What a travesty.

My dad's voice interrupted my fury. He said, "Don't dwell on that, Nancy. Just get her out of the dementia unit and give her the best time you can while you can."

He was right. I was going to maneuver her into the assisted living unit and get her a room to herself. She had always been a private person, and sharing space with dementia patients had been hard on her, especially since in their confusion they often helped themselves to Mother's clothes and personal items, and she could not stop them. After a tussle with the powers that be of the care home, who worried that she could not handle the change, I got Mother her own room. I hung her lovely paintings on the walls and ordered her a digital TV.

At first all this freedom frightened her. She remained in her room and would not come out for activities. One evening we sat together watching TV; Lady was with me that night, and she rested her head on Mother's feet.

"You know," Mother said, "I wasn't happy with you for a while because you put me in this room by myself. I was scared. I thought I had made you mad."

"Of course you didn't make me mad!" I answered. "I wanted you to be away from the dementia ward, to have your own things and see your paintings. Besides, you need to talk with people who are not confused."

She sighed happily. "That restaurant is nice. I go there to eat every day." She was smiling to herself. "I like the little patio outside my window too." She paused and sighed. "I just wish the view was better."

This was an opportunity to get her out of the room and I seized it. "Would you like to see an elegant view?"

"You know I would."

I wheeled my mother out of her room as she held Lady's leash. Lady was so well behaved that this was a safe arrangement. Wherever we went, Mother introduced us: "This is my dog Lady and my daughter Nancy. She takes care of Lady for me and brings her to visit." Such a rascal Mother was.

I pushed Mother's chair over to the windows in the activity area. At sunset, the sky blazed with color. The Allegheny Mountains looked like blue slate. She sat drinking in the view and patting Lady's big head until Lady melted down to the floor and fell asleep.

"Are we allowed to be out here?" Mother asked.

"Of course we are," I assured her. "This is like the living room for the place, and everyone is allowed here."

"I've missed having a view like this for so long," she sighed. "It reminds me of the apartment we had in Ecuador. Lovely!"

I watched her body relax and fear seemed to finally slip away from her shoulders.

For the rest of her life, unless I was on a business trip, we spent the evenings together, watching the sunset, or TV, and laughing and reminiscing.

Our favorite show in the last year of her life was *Dancing with the Stars*. Dancing had been such a great part of our lives, and we loved watching these wonderful performers competing. One night I cried when a couple did the Quickstep really well. "They are almost as good as you and Dad were, Mom," I said. "You and Daddy had that smoothness, like Astaire and Rogers. You were truly awesome."

She smiled and said, "Thank you. I never thought I was that good a dancer."

"You both were," I told her, "and it was a joy to watch you dancing through the house together. And when we went to parties, remember how the dance floor would clear when you and Dad performed some of the dances you grew up with?"

"Now that I do remember," she stated and then paused. "He was a wonderful man." We sat together cradling our memories.

In the years since his death, Mother had seen Dad only on rare occasions. Her psychic ability had never been as strong as mine, so most often she couldn't tell he was there, but now she began to see him every day.

"You know, your father came to see me today," she said during one of our visits.

"He did?" I said. "That was nice of him."

"Yes, he told me that I'm going home to live with him again soon."

She was content thinking about the idea; I was in shock. I knew he had been there, and I had no doubt about why he had told her such a thing—he had come to me a few days earlier to warn me that she didn't have much time left.

My mother said, "You have to promise me something."

I asked, "What do you need, Mom?"

She paused and said carefully, "When it comes time, and I can't go on with any kind of decent life here, let me go to be with him."

I nodded, and my tears fell.

"Promise me you will do that for me," she entreated.

I said, "I promise you that I will let you go when it's your time. I know you need to be with Dad again, and I'm glad he's there waiting for you."

For several more months I was able to enjoy my friendship with my Mother. She was so much herself, and she laughed and enjoyed teasing anyone in her line of vision. The staff had come to enjoy this sparkly, strong woman and stopped by often just to visit with her. She mentioned Dad every day now, and the staff told me she would come out of her room saying he had just been there. I assured them he was visiting her and she wasn't crazy—although the concept is difficult for non-psychic people to understand.

One particular evening, I was beat after a long day. I needed to decide if I was going to Spring Gardens to visit with Mother. As I ate a quick sandwich and ran through all my reasons for staying home, I heard my father's quiet tones, "You never know how much longer you'll be able to visit with her." He needed to say no more. I got my act together, prepared Lady, and we went for a visit.

Mother loved Lady and the feeling was mutual. Mother patted her and sat with that great blonde Labrador head in her lap and spoke sweetly to the dog. Finally, Lady collapsed in a heap, her head squarely on Mother's feet.

"I'm so glad you brought Lady," Mother said as she lazed in her chair. "I've been missing her, and I'm going to be leaving soon. I wanted to see her again."

I felt that familiar stinging in my eyes. I said, "I will miss you terribly when you go."

"I know, but this is no way for me to live," she swept her hand around the room. "You made it look nice with my paintings, but it's lonely here when you aren't visiting."

"I wish I could have made things better for you, Mom."

She looked right at me. "You have been wonderful, Nance. All the visits. Your kids. I don't know what I would have done without you."

We both cried a little, and then we buried ourselves in TV shows. Deep inside I knew she was saying goodbye. I understood she would be with Dad again and that would be much better, but I was going to have a hole in my heart. She was my mother and had become my best friend. I was so lucky to have had her all these years.

People think that being precognitive is a wonderful gift. Most of the time it is. I am usually braced when bad things happen, but the downside is knowing that someone's death is coming—especially someone whom I love dearly. It's a hard thing to keep what you'd call a "game face" on and proceed with life when I know someone I love is about to leave forever.

I drove home, trying to see the road through tears. I was so glad Dad warned me. I had a terrible feeling I would not see my mother alive again. It was just like the time I had seen my dad walk out my front door for the last time.

Sleep did not come that night. Lady sensed how upset I was and stayed in my bedroom, snoring on the floor next to my bed instead of retiring to her comfy quarters in the upstairs laundry room. Finally, I drifted off and awoke to sunlight trying to peek through my curtains. At least it was going to be a pretty day. I hustled to get ready for my drive to a local college where I was teaching, but I felt like my arms and legs were made of lead. Foreboding is an awful word, but it is the only one I can think of that describes the feeling I struggled with all day.

In the early afternoon the administrator from Spring Gardens called. "Your Mother's had a bad fall in the common room. We've called the ambulance. You need to come."

I raced to get Lady outside knowing I would not be back for a good long while. I called my daughter-in-law Rhonda, so that she could let Travis and Heidi know. Rhonda and Travis had been married since the summer of 1999. I knew that Mom was not going to survive. I wanted to get to her as fast as I could so she would not die alone.

I gave Susan a quick call on my cell and dashed to Latrobe Hospital's ER, where none of the staff knew about a Harriet Dankowski. They said she probably wasn't there yet. A few minutes later, however, a doctor came out to the waiting room to speak with me. He had treated my family many times before, and we knew each other well.

He told me, "Your mother is in critical condition. We don't have the neuro care she needs here. She was life-flighted to Pittsburgh."

I felt myself shaking, and my questions came rapid fire: "She's in a helicopter? What hospital did they take her to? Can you give me directions?"

As we hurried along, he said, "She never made it in to our ER. The paramedics called for life flight from wherever she was. If they thought she needed intensive care that fast, it isn't good. I'm sorry."

I had stuffed my pockets with tissues before I left home and I was glad I had. The doctor was on the phone trying to track down the helicopter and I stood right beside him, but I could not hear him. Instead, I heard rotor blades. Mother must have been at least partially conscious, because I knew I was picking up that sound from her.

Finally, the doctor hung up the phone and turned to me, "She's in the air on the way to Allegheny General. Do you know how to get to that hospital?"

Numbness had set in. I said I didn't, and one of the staff handed me directions. "Are you sure you can drive safely?" asked the doctor.

I pulled myself together. "I have handled disasters before. I can do this. But thank you for asking."

I knew that no one was close enough to help with the driving. I wanted to get to Allegheny General Hospital in Pittsburgh as fast as I could. As I got in the car, I noticed that the hospital phone number was listed on the directions. I called there to let them know I was Harriet Dankowski's daughter and was on the way. As I drove up the on-ramp to the turnpike, my cell phone rang. It was Allegheny General's ER social worker.

"Your mother has just arrived. We need to know some background on her."

I don't like to talk while I'm driving, so I answered her questions as fast as I could and added, "Tell her that Nancy is on the way and will be there soon."

It was a long 45 minutes until I arrived. I came to a desk, and a clerk who demanded that I fill out forms before I proceeded to the ER.

I said, "I have already talked with your social worker and given her the information you are asking for. She told me to come to the ER as soon as possible."

In the background, I heard a voice call, "Miss Myer, are you here yet?"

I turned to see an older woman looking around the waiting area. I called, "I'm Miss Myer! She won't let me go back to see my mother!"

The older woman turned a disgusted look on the clerk, "I told you to let me know when she got here. Come with me, Miss Myer. You can fill out paperwork later."

I entered the busy emergency area. When they opened the curtains to Mother's section, a doctor was talking to her. "Harriet, I think your daughter is here." He looked over at me. "What is your name?"

"Nancy."

"Harriet, Nancy is here."

Mother was surrounded by equipment, and I couldn't see her and she couldn't see me. "This won't do," I said, and the doctor shoved equipment around and made room for me to stand next to Mother.

The doctor said, "I need to watch her when you talk with her to see if she responds to you at all."

I asked, "Can I touch her?"

"Just reach around those tubes and touch her shoulder," the doctor directed. "Don't touch her head."

She lay with her eyes almost closed. Her face seemed to be badly bruised, and I wasn't sure if she was conscious.

"Mom, I'm here beside you. I'm going to look out for you." I patted her shoulder gently. Her eyes switched to me immediately. She had been looking down at her feet where she had heard my voice when I first entered the room.

"Good, she knows you," said the doctor.

Mother stared at me intently. From a great distance—in my head—I heard her call me. In response, I said aloud, "I'm right here, Mom." Her voice in my head became a little stronger. "Promise" was all she said.

I said, "I will keep my promise, Mom. I will look after you, but I will keep my promise."

She closed her eyes and a tear slid down her face. She never regained consciousness.

The doctors performed a procedure to relieve swelling in Mother's skull, and I sat in the waiting area while they did it. When the doctor finally came out to talk to me, seeing his face was all I needed to know things were really bad. "Your mother is no longer responding to any stimuli. The only reaction we saw since she arrived was when she reacted to your presence. She is being kept alive right now by the machines. You need to make a decision for her."

He went on, "If it's all right with you, I am going to run a brain scan within the hour."

I considered all he said. I told him, "I want to wait and see what the scan shows. I don't want to make a decision to stop life support until you are sure there is no hope. I need to be sure that I am letting her go, not killing her."

He smiled without meaning it and turned to go. "We will keep you informed about what's going on as it is happening. If you need anything, ask the social worker."

After he rushed off, I stared out the window at the sunny day and tried to get a grip on what was happening. The adrenalin that had gotten me to Pittsburgh was leaving my body, and a terrible let down set in.

An older lady near me in the waiting room brought me some juice, and we talked. The comfort offered by this stranger was heartwarming. She understood the terrible position I was in; I will always remember her kindness.

"I had to make this decision for my father," she explained. "Don't let them push you into it until you are ready." She went back to her family. I went back to staring into space. I remembered all the families I worked with during my career who had been in this same situation. They hired me to help them learn if there was any chance left. I had always been able to feel when the person's soul decided to let go and move on. Would I be able to recognize that moment with my own mother?

Inside I called out, "Let me know when, Mom." I heard nothing in return. So I sat for a lonely, long while until my kids arrived. It was wonderful having their support.

Mother had been moved to the Neuro ICU. My kids and I sat in a little waiting area just outside the door to the unit. As the day moved on, the reports on Mother's condition continued to be horrible. No response. No response at all.

Finally I said to the kids, "We need to go home and get some rest." Although we knew it was true, we were all reluctant to leave her. I went in to see her once more. I looked at her battered face and all the tubes. I still sensed a distant presence of her. All I wanted for her now was peace.

The drive home allowed me private time to gather strength. I went through the motions of letting Lady out and getting ready for bed. I lay there unable to relax. It was like the many nights after I had returned from Japan—feeling exhausted but being unable to sleep. I had the TV on more for company than anything else. The world felt empty without my mother's thought pattern. I remembered that same sense of emptiness when my Dad died so long ago.

Suddenly, a loud, insistent voice was calling: "Nancy! Nancy!"

I looked down at the foot of my bed. My mother and father were there together! Mother's soul had slipped free from her damaged body and Dad was there holding her again. I knew now that she had passed, and that the machines were prolonging the agony. Tears poured out of me as I saw how happy they were to be together after all this time. They glowed with love. Dad had his arms around Mother as she stood in front of him, and her arms were crossed over his, holding on tight. It seemed so natural to me that they were here to say goodbye.

Dad said, "It's her time, Nance. You need to be brave and let her go."

"Tell everyone I love them," said Mother.

Then they were gone.

I cried hard as I waited for the phone to ring bringing word from the hospital that she was gone. I glanced at the clock; it was 4:30 Thursday morning. When 6 a.m. rolled around and I still hadn't received a call, I picked up the phone and called them.

"Nothing has changed," said the voice in Neuro ICU. "No improvement. I'm sorry."

I had hoped she could go on her own, but that was not happening. Her soul was free, but her empty body remained trapped by the machines. I remembered the death of a dear friend several years earlier. Once the doctors told the family she could not be saved, she had remained trapped on life support for a time.

I thought about Mother's final word. "Promise."

As I walked Lady, fed her, and got dressed I knew that I would have to make the decision today. In fact, the decision already had been made by Mother. She was with my Dad now. Life support was impeding her soul's progress. I rode to the hospital with Travis and Rhonda. I filled them in on the early-morning visit from my parents and my call to the Neuro ICU. I wanted them to be prepared for the fact that we had to let her go.

Travis had not seen Mother the day before, and I went in to see her with him. This was the first time he was seeing a close relative die. None of my kids had been this close to death before. Back in the waiting room Travis and I sat while Heidi, Rhonda, and Diane, who later became Heidi's wife, visited Mother. I consider Diane and Rhonda my daughters too.

"It's not Guppy," said Travis to me. "She's not there, is she?"

"No, son," I said. "She's gone." There was no doubt of it today. Even the doctor and the nurses told me, "She's made her decision. She's gone. The only reason she's still breathing is because of life support." Her legs were swelling from the backup of fluid as her organs started to fail.

Late in the afternoon, I told the kids, "We have to say goodbye and then let them disconnect the machines."

At last the doctor sat down and explained, "Harriet as you knew her is gone. All her tests are showing no brain activity at all. She is breathing and being sustained by machines. It's time to make the decision."

The kids wanted to know what would happen next. He explained it and then turned to me and said, "Would you like me to disconnect her, and then you can visit with her once again so you can see her without all those tubes?"

I said, "Thank you. That would be helpful."

We waited while they took out the tubes and cleaned her up, and then we went to see her together. We stood with her, and we all let her know how much we loved her, that we knew she needed to be free of her body and this life. We went back to the waiting area and sat together talking and reminiscing.

Suddenly I heard her voice. "Go home and get some rest! I'm fine!"

I had the sense that she didn't want us to suffer through witnessing her death. I have felt this before—the dying person doesn't want family members to hear the last breath and keep that memory forever rather than focusing on all the good memories, so he or she waits until loved ones take a break and then expires when they aren't there.

We followed her instructions and went home. I got the call Friday morning at 4:35. She died at 4:30 a.m.—exactly 24 hours after she and Dad came to see me.

Mother was free and dancing with Dad at last.

Epilogue

The more that I learn from my father about life and death, the more I understand that I need to help others learn about all sides of existence. This is a difficult path. I have suffered hard lessons that some people do not think it's right, or even allowable, for a psychic to speak of God.

One publisher I had approached to help me tell my story railed at me, "Who the hell do you think you are to claim that your life was touched by God? Why would God even care about you?" The venom in her voice shocked me. She of course, was unaware she was espousing human judgments and not a point of view that God would be likely to agree with.

Her vicious remarks silenced me for a long time, but then I realized I could not allow someone like this to keep me silent. I knew that God felt I was worthy from my transformational experience in the Garden of Gethsemane. I made God a promise and no matter how uncomfortable it was, I needed to keep my promise. I had a responsibility to speak up and pray for strength when angry people like that publisher attacked.

What I have learned about life, death, and the Light of Life that God creates are things that I believe spiritual people can benefit from learning about. I hold firm to my belief that what I learned is important.

By seeking to understand all the stages of life, including death, I have found many answers that will help others to better understand the full journey of the soul—from birth to a return to God's light. I believe that

God exists in the form of light and an incredible love that accompanies that light. This knowledge gives me great peace.

The vacuum of Mother's absence is still with me. I expect it will be for a long time. She, like my father, has found it possible to contact me from the other side. She is quite adept at this communication, as she was well prepared for it by my dad's efforts. She has moved all kinds of objects in my house and at my son's and daughter's houses. A lot of the time what she does is funny, proving that her wonderful sense of humor survives.

We put together a collection of photos for her funeral service. The pictures included one of her riding on a Harley! That one was a hit as most of her relatives had no idea she was anywhere near a motorcycle. I am surrounded in my home by her wonderful paintings and the full aware-ness that my parents love me dearly even now.

I hear from them every now and then. They share in my joy and pride in my children and grandchildren. My grandson Trey's enthusiastic self has brought to them a lot of laughs just as he has to me. Mother and Dad were there when my granddaughter Kaitlyn was born, and they enjoy see-ing what a live wire she is.

They attended Heidi's graduation from college—something the doc-tors said she would never do. Heidi suffered a terrible head injury from a motor vehicle accident, but she is a lot like her grandmother and fought her way back to health and earned a Bachelor's degree. My parents watch in pride as Travis succeeds professionally and takes such good care of his family. They grieve with me that Blake and I are not in touch and that he still leads a troubled life.

They were there to greet Lady when she passed and to sit with me in prayer when Heidi had two more bouts with cancer. Their love and com-fort are always there. Their pride in their family and their love for all of us continues. I know that their souls continue to exist in this new way. While science works hard to say that after-death communication is just some kind of brain abnormality, I know they are wrong.

Mother and Dad are buried together in my dad's hometown. On their headstone, I had these words carved: "Death does not stop love." They are together now forever as they should be because, after all my psychic experiences with my father, my mother, and my own children, I know that nothing can stop real love, not even death.

Author's Note About Rose's Story

As I was writing this book, I realized that it was time to share the story of Rose and Lily so that both will be remembered as courageous young people tortured by madmen. When I typed the words into my computer, I described Rose as I remembered how she looked—I'd always thought she was a revered grandmother in that family. My editor pointed out, however, that Rose could not have been that old, considering her age when she was taken to the concentration camp, and asked me to revisit my memories of the story to see if I could remember anything else that would place her age more accurately.

I was about nine when I met Rose, and she was so scarred on her face, arms, and leg that she looked very old. She needed help to get in and out of her chair, and she walked slowly with a cane. Young children make assumptions about the adults around them, and that together with Rose's appearance made me believe she was much older than she must have been. I puzzled over my limited knowledge about her life.

My mother and father tried, from the other side, to help me understand that she was actually fairly young when I met her. She appeared so much older because of the suffering she had endured. In addition to the damage to her leg from the experiments, torture in the brothel from the soldiers scarred her face, arms, and hands and permanently damaged her inside so that she could never bear children, nor could she stand to be touched by men, other than the helping hands of family members. My parents had learned these details from the owner of the house we visited. It was a horrifying life that young Rose had led, but somehow she was strong enough to survive.

While talking with my parents' ghosts, I realized that the only clue we had to Rose's age was her statement that Lily was 12 when she died. She herself did not know how long they were in the camp before Lily died, as the agonizing existence they lived robbed them of the ability to keep track of time. I will never know exactly where she had been imprisoned or how long she had been there before the Allies liberated the camp. I only know that she had suffered more than any human being I have met in my life. I am sorry it took so long to find the forum in which to tell her story, so that Rose and Lily could be honored for the incredible courage they showed as children confronted by the insanity of a concentration camp built by Nazis.

Acknowledgments

This book would not be possible without my wonderfully adventurous, courageous, and loving parents who took me all over the world. I was not always a cooperative traveler, but they showed me the value of a world view, and I will always be grateful to them for giving me such an interesting childhood.

For many years, Tom Wettach, my attorney, provided knowledge to protect me. His quiet guidance is invaluable. I will always be grateful for his wise words and velvet-fisted letters when I needed them most. Thank you, Tom, for being an able lawyer and a good friend.

I just learned of the passing of my friend and mentor Col. Irvin B. Smith, Delaware State Police (Ret.). I met him as my career started, and he convinced me to try my skills at solving murders. He had great faith that my talents would be invaluable in police work. I was not so sure but caved after his polite police harassment and we became colleagues and friends. I will miss him. Thank you, Smitty, for convincing me to try police work.

My publishers Robert and Mary Matzen saw the tiny beginning of my book and bought it, to my amazement. Through the last year, they questioned me over and over, asking me to explain terms like ranging, until the book evolved into something worth reading. They also insisted that I do something I was not comfortable doing. They asked me to stop being so reserved and to add my emotions into the story as they were convinced that there was no story without that input. Of course, they were right, but that was hard for me.

My children, Travis, Heidi, and Blake, have had to put up with their mom's unusual profession. They never knew anything else, but I am aware that they experienced bullying for having such an unusual mother. I greatly regret that, and I am especially saddened because most of the bullies were adults! I would like to honor my children's courage and strength to stand up to what they went through. I am proud of all of you, and I have nothing in my life that brings me greater pleasure than being your mother. I'd also like to include my daughters by marriage, Rhonda Anderson and Diane Anderson, in my thanks as they have added new ideas and voices, and shared with me their lovely children in order of youngest to oldest: Kaitlyn, Trey, Sarah, and Josh. I have one more grandson that I have not had much opportunity to get to know, Blake, Jr. I really love being a grandmother.

My sister, Susan Scott, and her daughters, Laurie and Tracy, and their families have also lent encouragement to my efforts. My other nieces and nephew, Diane, Arden, and David, and their beautiful families added their share of fun and enjoyment to my life as well.

I do not forget all the brave detectives I've worked with over the years. They took a lot of teasing for working with me but enjoyed the last laugh when the cases were solved one after another: Col. Smith, now gone; Gregory Sacco, Delaware State Police; and the whole Sherlock Squad. I remember the fun we had and the cases we worked so well. I treasure the nickname, Lady Sherlock, that they gave me.

The Wilmington (Delaware) Police Department worked with me for years. My unofficial partners were Detectives Leroy Landon, now gone, and Jay Ingraham. Tony Rispoli and Ed Head were on the same shift, and also and worked many of the cases with us. Even though they claimed I threw up in their squad car when I didn't, it was wonderful working with them. I have fond memories of the many cases we worked and solved together.

All these men and women helped me to figure out how to do my job most effectively, and although I worked with many detectives after them, I remember the first group best as we learned together how to do the job right. Of course, they all had to pull tricks on me and others, but that kept me laughing when I would otherwise have cried at the nightmares I visualized. I also appreciated their protective presence when things got hairy. All of them helped me learn to survive seeing the worst of humanity, yet come away with faith in the better part of humanity. When they worked 24 hours a day on cases and gave up their free time to stop killers, they showed the best of humanity. I see the best of what police detectives do, and I honor their incredible skill, courage, and determination.

I would be remiss if I did not recognize the Writing Popular Fiction program and my teachers at Seton Hill University in Greensburg, Pennsylvania. Albert Wendland, Ph.D., Lee McClain, Ph.D., and Michael Arnzen, Ph.D. Their training turned me into a much better writer than I expected to be. I would also like to thank Lisa Carino and Mary Cox, from the alumni office, with whom I worked to start the yearly seminar, "In Your Write Mind." Thank you, Seton Hill University, for having such a great writing program.

I would also like to thank two author friends of mine, Lois Duncan and Leslie Rule, who agreed to review my book. I admire their writing and I appreciate that they are doing this for me. Jay Ingraham and Tony Rispoli, detectives I worked with for years, also reviewed the book. Thank you for being there for me.

My life has been a wonderful journey, and I am lucky to have shared it with many other people. Unfortunately, space does not allow me to mention all those people individually, but I value every one of them. To all who touched my life and wished me onward, I offer my thanks, because no one prospers in life without the help of many.

Nancy Myer
July 2013